PALATKA
ST. JOHNS RIVER
OKLAWAHA RIVER
EUREKA
LAKE GEORGE
FT. VOLUSIA
JUNIPER SPRINGS
Robert E. Carson

Frontier Eden

Checklist of Publications

The following list of publications is selective. It is meant to indicate the main format of Marjorie Kinnan Rawlings' literary career and excludes juvenilia, the pre-Florida journalistic writings, and most reprints.

BOOKS

South Moon Under, New York, 1933.
Golden Apples, New York, 1935.
The Yearling, New York, 1938.
When the Whippoorwill, New York, 1940.
Cross Creek, New York, 1942.
Cross Creek Cookery, New York, 1942.
Jacob's Ladder, Miami, Florida, 1950.
The Sojourner, New York, 1953.
Secret River, New York, 1955.
The Marjorie Rawlings Reader, ed. Julia Scribner Bigham, New York, 1956.

SHORT STORIES

"Cracker Chidlings," *Scribner's*, LXXXIX (February 1931), 127–34.
"Jacob's Ladder," *Scribner's*, LXXXIX (April 1931), 351–66, 446–64.
"Plumb Clare Conscience," *Scribner's*, LXXXX (December 1931), 622–26.
"Crop of Beans," *Scribner's*, LXXXXI (May 1932), 283–90.
"Gal Young Un," *Harper's*, CLXV (June 1932), 21–33; (July 1932), 225–34.

"Alligators" [with Fred Tompkins], *Saturday Evening Post,* CCVI (September 23, 1933), 16 ff.
"Benny and the Bird Dogs," *Scribner's,* LXXXIV (October 1933), 193–200.
"The Pardon," *Scribner's,* LXXXXVI (August 1934), 95–98.
"Varmints," *Scribner's,* C (November 1963), 26–32.
"A Mother in Mannville," *Saturday Evening Post,* CCIX (December 12, 1936), 7 ff.
"Cocks Must Crow," *Saturday Evening Post,* CCXII (November 25, 1939), 5 ff.
"The Pelican's Shadow," *New Yorker,* XV (January 6, 1940), 17–19.
"The Enemy," *Saturday Evening Post,* CCXXII (January 20, 1940), 12 ff.
"In the Heart," *Collier's,* CV (February 3, 1940), 19 ff.
"Jessamine Springs," *New Yorker,* XVII (February 22, 1941), 19 ff.
"Provider," *Woman's Home Companion,* LXVIII (June 1941), 20 ff.
"Shell," *New Yorker,* XX (December 9, 1944), 29 ff.
"Black Secret," *New Yorker,* XXI (September 8, 1945), 20 ff.
"Miriam's Houses," *New Yorker,* XXI (November 25, 1945), 24 ff.
"Mountain Prelude," *Saturday Evening Post,* CCXIX (April 26, 1947), 10 ff; (May 3, 1947), 36 ff.; (May 10, 1947), 38 ff.; (May 17, 1947), 40 ff.; (May 24, 1947), 36 ff.; (May 31, 1947), 40 ff. [A novel published serially; never published in book form.]
"Friendship," *Saturday Evening Post,* CCXXI (January 1, 1949), 14 ff.

POEMS

"Having Left Cities Behind Me," *Scribner's,* LXXXXVIII (October 1935), 246.
"Mountain Rain," *Scribner's,* CIV (July 1938), 63.

NON-FICTION PROSE

"Hyacinth Drift," *Scribner's,* LXXXXIV (September 1933), 164–73.
"I Sing While I Cook," *Vogue,* XCIII (February 15, 1939), 48.
"Regional Literature of the South," *College English,* I (February 1940), 381–89.
"Here Is Home," *Atlantic,* CLXIX (March 1942), 277–85.

"Who Owns Cross Creek?" *Atlantic*, CLXIX (April 1942), 439–50.
"Fanny–You Fool!" *Vogue*, C (July 15, 1942), 42.
"Sweet Talk, Honey!" *Vogue*, C (December 1, 1942), 77.
"Cross Creek Breakfasts," *Woman's Home Companion*, LXIX (November 1942), 72 ff.
"Trees for Tomorrow," *Collier's*, CXVII (May 8, 1943), 14 ff.
"Florida: A Land of Contrasts," *Transatlantic*, XIV (October 1944), 12–17.
"Introduction," *Katherine Mansfield Collection*, ed. John Middleton Murry, Cleveland, 1946.
"Writing as a Career," *The Book of Knowledge*, 1948 Annual Supplement.
"Portrait of a Magnificent Editor as Seen in His Letters," *Publishers' Weekly*, CLVII (April 1, 1950), 1573 ff.

* * *

Published scholarly writing about Mrs. Rawlings is sparse. Numerous brief reviews of her books exist; there is a scattering of human interest feature articles on such occasions as her receiving the Pulitzer Prize; and there are factual summaries in the standard reference sources. But on the whole Mrs. Rawlings and her career have received little notice, even by the literary histories and studies of regional literature. The exceptions can be briefly given: Harry Bernard, *Le Roman Régionaliste aux Etats-Unis, 1913–1940*, Montreal, 1949; M. G. Figh, "Folklore and Folk Speech in the Works of Marjorie Kinnan Rawlings," *Southern Folklore Quarterly*, XI (September, 1947), 201–209; L. Morris, "New Classicist," *North American Review*, CCXXXXVI (September, 1938), 179–84.

The University of Florida Library contains five manuscript studies of Mrs. Rawlings: Ambolena H. Robillard, *Maxwell Evarts Perkins: the Author's Editor*, doctoral dissertation, 1954; Carl Tim Furlow, *Folklore Elements in the Florida Writings of Marjorie Kinnan Rawlings*, Master's thesis, 1963; William J. McGuire, *A Study of Florida Cracker Dialect Based Chiefly on the Prose Works of Marjorie Kinnan Rawlings*, Master's thesis, 1939; Joseph R. Peck, *The Fiction-Writing Art of Marjorie Kinnan Rawlings*, Master's thesis, 1954; Mary Louise Slagle, *The Artistic Uses of Nature in the Fiction of Marjorie Kinnan Rawlings*, Master's thesis, 1953.

Chronology

1896 Born August 8, Washington, D.C. Her father, Arthur Frank Kinnan, an examiner in the U.S. Patent Office; her mother, Ida May Traphagen Kinnan.

1907 Wins a $2.00 prize for a story published in the Washington *Post.*

1913 Father dies.

1914 June, graduates from Western High School in Washington. Mother moves with Marjorie and younger brother Arthur to Madison, Wisconsin. September, Marjorie enters University of Wisconsin as an English major.

1918 Graduates from University of Wisconsin (Phi Beta Kappa in Junior year). Moves to New York City; works as an editor for the National Board of the YWCA.

1919 May, marries Charles A. Rawlings; takes up residence in his home city of Rochester.

1920–1928 MKR a feature writer for the Louisville *Courier-Journal* and the Rochester *Journal-American.* Writes daily syndicated feature, "Songs of the Housewife," May 1926 to February 1928. Works continually on short fiction but unable to publish.

1928 March, first trip to Florida. Buys Cross Creek grove property in late summer and moves to Florida in early November.

1929 Immediately begins to record impressions of countryside and Florida people.

1930 March, sells first story, "Cracker Chidlings," to *Scribner's* for $150. December, sells second story, "Jacob's Ladder," to *Scribner's* for $700. Becomes protégé of Maxwell Perkins.

1931 "Cracker Chidlings" published in February issue of *Scribner's;* "Jacob's Ladder" published in April issue. August to October, lives in the Big Scrub with the Fiddia family.

1932 Continues to publish short fiction on Florida subjects. Now working on first novel of the Big Scrub.

1933 March, *South Moon Under* published, an immediate critical and popular success. June, first mention of *The Yearling* in an exchange of letters with Maxwell Perkins. July, lives with family of Cal Long in the Big Scrub, gathering material for *The Yearling.* August to September, voyage to England. November, divorce from Charles Rawlings made final. Receives $500 O. Henry Award for "Gal Young Un."

1934 December, completes draft of *Golden Apples* after severe struggle. Cut version of book sold to *Cosmopolitan.*

1935 February, breaks neck in fall from horse; wearing neck brace, completes revisions of *Golden Apples.* August, visits brother Arthur in Seattle. Takes boat trip on Inland Waterway to Alaska.

1936 May, meets Hemingway in Bimini. June-July, hunts bear in Big Scrub with Barney Dillard. September, begins writing *The Yearling* in mountain cabin at Banner Elk, North Carolina. October, meets Fitzgerald at Grove Park Inn, Asheville.

1937 June, drives to New York City with partial version of novel. Perkins introduces her to Thomas Wolfe.

1938 February, *The Yearling* published; April, film rights sold to MGM for $30,000. Book becomes a major best-seller and MKR begins to be a national celebrity.

1939 January, elected to National Academy of Arts and Letters. May, receives the Pulitzer Prize for fiction. Begins research for book on Zephaniah Kingsley, an eccentric early 19th-century Florida planter.

1940 March, *When the Whippoorwill,* a collection of short stories, is published. Abandons Kingsley novel and begins work on *Cross Creek.*

1941 May, MGM begins production of movie version of *The*

Yearling on location in the Big Scrub. October, completes writing of *Cross Creek.* Marries Norton Sanford Baskin, manager of Castle Warden Hotel, St. Augustine. Moves from Cross Creek to St. Augustine.

1942 February, *Cross Creek* published, another major best-seller. May, awarded Doctor of Humane Letters by the University of Florida. August, *Cross Creek Cookery* published.

1943 January, Zelma Cason enters $100,000 suit against MKR for libel. June, begins work on a novel based on her grandfather Traphagen (*The Sojourner*).

1944 Begins massive correspondence with American servicemen. In spite of repeated starts, novel goes badly. June, Florida Supreme Court rules that grounds for suit exist if charge is changed from libel to "invasion of privacy."

1945 Continues to labor over *The Sojourner.* Continues to publish short fiction, but stories are based less and less on Florida material.

1946 May, "Cross Creek Trial" held in Gainesville, Florida. MKR wins decision, but Zelma Cason appeals and case goes a second time to the state Supreme Court.

1947 May, Florida Supreme Court reverses decision of circuit court in a 3–4 decision, directing that MKR pay nominal damages of one dollar and costs. June, MKR spends summer in Van Hornesville, New York, in cottage lent by Owen D. Young. Told of Maxwell Perkins' death. Buys and renovates old farmhouse in Van Hornesville. Novel *Mountain Prelude* serialized in *Saturday Evening Post.*

1952 February, suffers coronary heart attack while alone in house at Cross Creek. Recovers, and continues labor on *The Sojourner*, which is finally completed in August.

1953 January, *The Sojourner* published; adopted by Literary Guild, but receives lukewarm critical response. February, begins research for biography of Ellen Glasgow. In Richmond for several months to gather data. December 14, dies of a cerebral hemorrhage at Crescent Beach, Florida. Buried in Antioch Cemetery near Island Grove, Florida.

The Literary Career of Marjorie Kinnan Rawlings

University of Florida Press
Gainesville

FRONTIER EDEN

by GORDON E. BIGELOW

For Lydia

A University of Florida Press Book

Third Impression, 1972

Library of Congress Catalog Card No. 66–26808

LITHO PRINTED IN FLORIDA

Contents

Preface

IN THE 1840's Herman Melville achieved sudden literary fame with a novel called *Typee*, which was a fictionalized account of his adventures among Polynesian natives on an Edenic tropical island of the Marquesas group. His fame was due at first almost as much to his striking experience as it was to the literary performance itself, so that he was celebrated not only as a man of letters but also as "the man who lived among cannibals." In the 1930's Marjorie Kinnan Rawlings achieved sudden literary fame for similar reasons. She wrote a series of books based on her adventures in a little-known semitropical world of north central Florida. As in Melville's case, it may have been the books which attracted attention to her, but behind the books was a personal experience which held the imagination, and for years Marjorie registered in the public consciousness not only as an accomplished writer but as "the woman who lived among the crackers."

In this present book about her—the first extensive study of her life or work—I have tried to present a valid portrait of the colorful person who made good her escape to Eden, but my chief emphasis has been upon the writings, and biography here has been made to serve the ends of literary criticism. Her writings were after all the most significant aspect of an interesting life, and literary fame was the only kind of fame she herself had any desire for or any real respect for. This emphasis has seemed the more justifiable because her work has suffered an almost total neglect by critics and, although America's literature in the present century is unusually rich, it is not so rich that writings as good as her best should suffer this kind of neglect indefinitely. My intention has been to describe what she did as a writer, to assess her strengths and weaknesses as a literary artist, and to relate her writings to her time and to the stream of literary history. Under this kind of scrutiny she held up very well—grew larger rather than smaller. Close study not only confirmed that she had substantial merit as a Florida regionalist and comic writer, but also showed that her books have an unexpected depth of theme and idea, and that they represent a significant contribution to the American pastoral tradition.

This book is meant to be scholarly in the sense that I have tried to gather all the facts I could find and to be scrupulously faithful to them, but I have tried to avoid its becoming an "academic" book and have kept the scholarly machinery as much as possible out of view. The research for this book was fascinating. When I first told my wife that I meant to write a book about Marjorie Kinnan Rawlings, she said, "That's fine. I'll get you a shotgun for your birthday," under the sound notion that if I was going to do a book of this sort then one kind of preparation for it should be to learn as much as possible about outdoor life in this part of Florida. So bird-shooting became one form of "research," and an airboat excursion on Orange Lake at night to gig frogs, and an expedition to Salt Springs to spear blue crabs in the run, and alligator-tail steak in a fish-camp restaurant at Cross Creek, and tramping through the Ocala Scrub, and canoe trips on the Oklawaha to look for Taylor's Dread and on

Juniper Springs Run to see the place where Ol' Slewfoot was killed. This was a kind of thing I had been doing in the area for years. The Rawlings project quite literally combined business with pleasure by giving such activities new focus.

A second phase of research, a little less exotic but equally interesting, involved interviewing people who had known Marjorie, and visiting places that were of importance to her life or writings. This trail naturally crisscrossed central Florida many times, with nodes of concentration in the Cross Creek area, the scrub, and St. Augustine. In the spring of 1961, aided by travel funds from The American Philosophical Society and the Graduate School of the University of Florida, I followed the trail to many places outside of Florida, including Washington, D. C.; New York City; Damariscotta Mills, Maine; Van Hornesville and Rochester in upper New York State; Madison, Wisconsin; Louisville, Kentucky; and Atlanta, Georgia.

A third phase of research involved prolonged study of the large collection of Rawlings letters and papers in the University of Florida Library. This collection was established by Marjorie's own donation of manuscripts in 1950 and was subsequently greatly enlarged by the faithful efforts of her literary executrix, Mrs. Julia Scribner Bigham, and by the generous response of many of Marjorie's correspondents to a canvass begun as part of this present project.

Any book of this sort is perforce a collaboration, and among the many persons to whom I am indebted for interview or for letters or for other assistance, I should like to mention first Mrs. Bigham, who on several occasions gave graciously of her time for interview and who, before her tragic death of cancer in 1962, saw that copies of Marjorie's side of the Rawlings-Perkins correspondence and several large boxes of manuscripts and letters left in her care were added to the collection in the University of Florida Library. Without these materials this present book would have been much thinner. My debt to Mr. Norton Baskin of St. Augustine, Florida, can best be expressed by saying that after more than four years of answering innumerable queries he has continued to be so cordial that I think of him as a valued personal friend. One of the highlights of the long research trip in 1961 was a two-day interview with Mr. Charles A. Rawlings, during which with great candor and good will he provided invaluable information on Marjorie's university days, on the Rochester years, and the early years at Cross Creek. I am indebted also to Mrs. Dorothy Benton Ruffner, for information on Marjorie's Rochester years; to Professor and Mrs. Clifford P. Lyons, for personalia and for information about the late thirties and the Cross Creek Trial; to "Aunt" Martha and "Uncle" Will Mickens, for interesting material on the Cross Creek years; to Mr. Carl Van Vechten, for perceptive comments on Marjorie's late years, for the donation of a sprightly correspondence and a series of photographic portraits to the Rawlings Collection; to Mr. and Mrs. Walter Gilkyson, for warm hospitality, for many valuable letters and good talk about many aspects of Marjorie's career; to Miss Esther Forbes, for much information on the college years, and particularly her activities with the University of Wisconsin *Lit;* to the Juniper Club and particularly Mr. H. L. Nevin for a memorable night at the clubhouse and to Mr. Russell Mattox for a guided tour of *The Yearling* country; to Mr. "Pat" Townsend for an unforgettable frog-hunt on Orange Lake; to Mr. Chet Crosby, for a tour of Marjorie's bird-hunting grounds; to Mr. Richard Mills and Mr. James Duke of the Lake Bryant Ranger Station in the Ocala National Forest for a most cordial tour of the scrub country and for valuable talk about the geography and geology and history of the scrub; to Mrs. Dessie Smith Prescott, for vivid reminiscence on many aspects of the Cross Creek years; to Cathy Alsop and Ron Sherman for pleasant excursions with camera and notebook in the Cross Creek area; and to Ron Sherman again for permission to use several of his photographs. Special thanks are due to my long-time colleague and friend, Dr. Robert E. Carson. The excellent ink drawings which embellish the book are testimony enough to his artistic talent, though they hardly can say the word which should be said about his spirit of generous and friendly cooperation.

For letters or interviews or courtesies of many kinds I should also like to thank the following: H. J. Bernhardt, Harold W. Blodgett, Philip Booth, Margaret Freeman Cabell, Zelma Cason, Henry R. Clune, Mark Ethridge, Mrs. J. F. Defandorf, Mrs. W. H. Draper, Jr., Lillian Gilkes, Helen King Hastings, Scott H. Goodnight, Mrs. Hanna Josephson, Arthur Kinnan, Grace Kinnan, Mr. and Mrs. Philip May, Beatrice Humiston McNeill, Marguerite Morris, Max C. Otto, Edith Pope, Theodore Pratt, Professor and Mrs. C. A. Robertson, D. L. Scott, Edwin Way Teale, Douglas Watson, Mrs. Frank Lloyd Weaver.

Without libraries and librarians the literary researcher would be helpless, and I owe many courtesies to the staffs of the Rochester Public Library, the University of Wisconsin Library, and above all the University of Florida Library. Several persons there deserve special mention: Mr. Stanley L. West, Director of Libraries, who knew Marjorie well and had an important personal role in the acquisition of several parts of the Rawlings Collection; Mr. John Buechler, former head of Special Collections, who helped me rescue from jeopardy a large number of Marjorie's books, letters, and manuscripts; Miss Laura Monti, present head of Special Collections, who catalogued and put in order most of the Rawlings papers and whose patient help and interest over several years have shown her to be a very gem among librarians.

Two of my colleagues, Professors Robert A. Bryan and Harry R. Warfel, generously took time from busy schedules to read the completed manuscript and make perceptive and helpful suggestions. Portions of chapters 4 and 5 relating to the wilderness theme have appeared in different form in *Sewanee Review*, LXXIII, No. 2 (Spring, 1965).

G. E. B.

ABBREVIATIONS USED IN THE TEXTUAL NOTES:

SMU for *South Moon Under*
GA for *Golden Apples*
Y for *The Yearling*
WTW for *When the Whippoorwill*
CC for *Cross Creek*
CCC for *Cross Creek Cookery*
Soj for *The Sojourner*
Cr Ch for "Cracker Chidlings"

Letters have been cited by use of initials and date, e.g. [MKR to MEP May 13, 1938] means Marjorie Kinnan Rawlings to Maxwell E. Perkins, May 13, 1938.

Unless otherwise noted, all letters and MSS cited are part of the MARJORIE KINNAN RAWLINGS COLLECTION in the University of Florida Library.

1

The Long Road Up

MARJORIE KINNAN RAWLINGS belongs to the great renaissance in American fiction between the two World Wars. She was a meticulous artist with high standards who worked hard and, though her output was modest, her best work has an excellence which tempts one to the word "classic"; but she was so surrounded by other literary giants that her accomplishment has been obscured by theirs. Her major themes and attitudes place her squarely in one of the mainstreams of American culture, and yet she belonged to none of the literary schools or groupings of the period in which she wrote, unless it is to the regionalists and their rediscovery of the beauty and worth of the American scene as a subject for literature.

As a protégé of Maxwell Perkins, the great editor at Scribner's, she belonged to a literary elite which included Wolfe, Hemingway, and Fitzgerald, all of whom she knew. In terms of age she might have qualified as a member of the Lost Generation for her birth year was 1896, which made her three years older than Hemingway, a year older than Faulkner, and the same age as Fitzgerald and Dos Passos, but for several reasons she remains distinct from them all. As a female, she missed military service in World War I and the European exile which was its sequel for so many American writers and, though she was a dedicated writer from an early age, her literary career was slower getting started by a full decade than for most of her distinguished contemporaries. Her important writings appeared during the thirties and early forties but reflect very little of the prevailing naturalism or social consciousness of those years. She wrote of poor-whites in an exotic, semitropical setting, with unusual candor and lucidity but without showing them as the victims of corrupt capitalism or as depraved moral degenerates. Her books have little of the iconoclasm or pessimism of the time; without being sentimental they are mainly affirmative in tone. Though she made little use of sex, physical violence, or sensation, her books enjoyed an enormous popular success, selling so well in the years just before World War II that she became something of a national celebrity. Her writings brought her a number of awards and honors, including the O. Henry First Prize Award in 1933, the Pulitzer Prize for fiction in 1939, and three honorary doctorates; her best-known novel, *The Yearling*, was translated into thirteen languages and acclaimed as a literary masterpiece in many parts of the world. Since she was chiefly a plain-spoken writer, not a conscious symbolist except in her last novel, she has attracted little attention from critics interested in ironies, ambiguities, and symbol-chasing.

Her mature life and literary career can be understood only in terms of her discovery of Florida in 1928, and this was for her as much as for Ponce de Leon four centuries earlier, a true discovery. As some novelists are preoccupied with people, with the action and interaction of human character in a social context, Marjorie Rawlings was stirred by place. She habitually looked at people as they related to their setting and was convinced that this relationship was as radical as any relationship between people. She had a touch of the Indian or hamadryad in her. Like Thoreau she *felt* the life in plants, the spirit of a river or of a great storm. She felt also that places quite as much as people have a definite character or personality, and that just as a man has an affinity for some persons and not for others he also has an affinity for some places and not for others. She felt that it would be difficult for a man to find happiness until he found a place with which his spirit could live in harmony, and that for a man to live where he was out of harmony with his surroundings would lead to a frustration amounting to a kind of death. The place which was to be her soul's mate she found only after half her life was over and then almost by accident.

She had her first glimpse of Florida from the deck of a Clyde Line steamer as the ship nosed into the mouth of the St. Johns River from the Atlantic in March of 1928. She and her husband Charles Rawlings had taken a vacation from newspaper jobs in Rochester and had booked passage from New York to Jacksonville, intending to combine a holiday in Florida with the pleasure of an ocean cruise. During the two-day passage, they had watched the sky change from heavy overcast to bright blue, the sea from gray to brilliant green, and then on the morning of the second day the ship headed into a river whose waters were dark brown and more than a mile wide. They could see the alien silhouette of palm trees against the sky and the low line of salt marshes. They were met in Jacksonville by a brusque, pert woman named Zelma Cason who took them to a hotel south of the city on the bank of the St. Johns. As they watched the great river sweep past, smelling dark and tropical like a river out of Conrad, they turned to one another. Marjorie said, "Let's sell everything and move South. How we could write!" Much of the motive behind these words was sheer impulse, but there were deeper reasons as well, some of which stretched far back into her childhood. As it turned out, she and Charles did exactly what her impulsive words described.

Charles' two brothers, Wray and James, had been in Florida for several years, dabbling in real estate after the collapse of the Florida boom, and were living in the center of the state in the little town of Island Grove on the northern fringe of the citrus country. With the Rawlings brothers as guides, Marjorie and Charles saw much of this area during the next week—tramped in the wilderness area known as the Ocala Scrub, fished on Orange Lake, took a boat trip on the marvelously beautiful Oklawaha River. When it was time to return to Rochester, their minds were definitely made up; they asked Wray and James to look for a citrus grove property which could support them while they tried to write. Marjorie had inherited a few thousand dollars from her mother, part of the proceeds from the sale of a dairy farm her father had owned on the outskirts of Washington, D. C. Added to what they could get from selling their house in Rochester, this would provide enough for a down payment and a small capital to get them started.

In July, Wray wired to Rochester that he had found a place—seventy-four acres of hammock land planted mainly to citrus, lying four miles west of Island Grove in a tiny hamlet called Cross Creek. For $7,400 down and a mortgage for $7,000 more they could buy seventy-four acres of land with three thousand bearing citrus trees, a small pecan grove, some unused acres which could be planted to winter truck crops, a flock of two hundred chickens, chicken houses, farm implements, two mules, a battered Ford truck, a barn, a four-room tenant house, and an eight-room farmhouse. Marjorie sent a check to close the sale; she and Charles wound up their affairs in Rochester and in early November of 1928 moved to Florida.

When she first saw the grove and the old farmhouse, she felt, as she later wrote, not only love but terror, "such as one feels in the first recognition of a human love, for the joining of person to place, as of person to person, is a commitment to shared sorrow, even as to shared joy." When she stepped for the first time out of the bright sunlight into the deep shade of the orange grove, she had a feeling that after long years of spiritual homelessness she had at last come home, that an old thread, long tangled, had come straight.

Of the deeper motives which brought Marjorie to Cross Creek, one is perfectly understandable to many Americans who still cherish an instinct inherited from emigrant or frontiersman forbears, the instinct to flee the cramp and jostle of life in cities and "light out for the territory." Marjorie was one of the few who do more to satisfy this urge than to buy a summer place in the country. With typically headlong enthusiasm, after living thirty-two years in northern cities, she struck out clear to the subtropics, to an orange grove lying in a half-wild jungle area between two great marshy lakes in central Florida. The wildness and remoteness were part of the attraction. That she chose this kind of escape rather than flight to the boulevards and cafes of Paris, like so many other writers of the time, may have been due to blood inheritance. At the time she bought the property, an aunt, her father's sister, wrote her that she must have inherited "that fatal drop of Pearce blood, clamoring for change and adventure, and above all, for a farm. I never knew a Pearce who didn't secretly long for a farm." Marjorie's father had been an attorney with an important position in the U. S. Patent Office in Washington and raised his family in the pleasant suburb of Brooklandville, but his heart was in a farm he owned in Maryland just outside the city, where he often took Marjorie for long rambles through the countryside. During the summer the whole family lived in tents in a locust grove on the farm which was surrounded by a strand or two of barbed wire to keep the grazing cattle from moving too close. Marjorie and her younger brother Arthur roamed the fields and woods and fished for tiny, almost uncatchable fish in the clear brook which ran through the property. She always attributed her deep love of nature to the long summers on this Maryland farm and to visits to her grandfather Traphagen's farm in Michigan.

But Marjorie *lived* in the city and went to the Washington public schools, where in the early grades she felt the first stirring of the writer's "sweet hell within." When she was seventeen, just completing high school, her beloved father died, and her mother, influenced by the family friendship with the La Follettes, moved to Madison, Wisconsin, where she established a home so that Marjorie and her brother could attend the University of Wisconsin. Marjorie entered as an English major in

September of 1914 and showed quickness, if not brilliance, as a student. She was elected to Phi Beta Kappa while still a junior. She also entered into a whirlwind of extracurricular activities, particularly those involving writing and dramatics, and quickly became one of the most active of an unusually talented group who wrote and edited the campus literary magazine. Shortly after graduation in 1918 she went to New York City, almost the proverbial green kid from the sticks—slim, attractive, with sixty dollars, a satchel full of poems and stories she had written at the university, and the scared confidence that these would soon prove the means of finding her a job in the publishing world. Soon after her arrival in the big city a thief stole all her money. Years later she made the wry comment that this must have been an unusually discerning thief since he took only the money and left untouched the manuscripts which were in the same satchel, but at the time it was a terrible blow. She was rescued by Signe Toksvig at the *New Republic*, who dried her tears and lent her twenty dollars, enough to tide her over until she found a place doing editorial work for the National Board of the YWCA.

Since leaving Madison she had been keeping in almost daily contact by letter with Charles Rawlings, whom she had known as a fellow member of the Wisconsin *Lit* staff. She and Charles were married in May of 1919 and moved to his home city of Rochester. For a year or two Charles tried a heartbreaking pursuit of quick commercial success, first as publicity agent for a New York import-export firm, only to see the firm collapse shortly after his joining it. Then he went on the road, traveling a circuit of the big middle western cities as a salesman for a Rochester shoe company his father partly owned, while Marjorie stayed at home writing poetry and stories which she tried without success to sell to the slick magazines. Charles had no talent for sales and soon gave up the job, which he hated, and both turned to newspaper work, first in Louisville and then in Rochester, he as a reporter with a specialty in Great Lakes yachting events, she as a feature writer for the Sunday supplements and as a syndicated "poetess."

She always claimed that her newspaper years taught her more about writing than she had learned in all her university classes in writing or all her experience on the Wisconsin *Lit*, because in the hard school of reporting she learned to abandon the purple prose dear to all young writers and to tell a straight simple story. This was her later recollection; the feature articles themselves tell a somewhat different story. They read much like conventional Sunday supplement journalism: an account of a love-triangle murder told so as to squeeze out the last lurid sensation; an interview with movie star Lou Tellegen written in simpering women's page style; a coy account of two Mt. Holyoke students expelled because they refused to give up smoking cigarettes and wearing knickers. She may have been amusing herself by spoofing the excesses of Hearst journalism, but there is little in any of her newspaper writing from which one could predict the sensitive, lyric beauty of her best Florida stories. There is even less in her syndicated poems.

Each day except Sunday, from May 24, 1926, to February 29, 1928, Marjorie wrote one of the "Songs of the Housewife," a feature which started modestly in the Rochester *Times-Union* but which was soon picked up by the McClure Syndicate and eventually had a circulation of some fifty newspapers. An editorial note published with the first poem rhapsodically explains her intention: "Marjorie Rawlings tells of the joys, of the accomplishments; hers are the songs of satisfaction. She has found the romance of the dishpan and kettle. She is the first of all newspaper column writers who has glorified the housewife." These poems were uniformly cheery, sentimental pieces about little boys who tracked dirt across mother's clean floors on the way to the cookie jar, about the clean, sweet smell of laundry just taken from the line, about the beauty of sunlight streaming through the kitchen window and making rainbows in the soap suds of the dishpan. Considering that her own marriage was childless, that she was not a particularly good housewife, not even the cook of genius she was later to become, her success with this series is remarkable, chiefly as a testimony to her ingenuity and perseverance. She did her daily stint with as good faith as she could muster, but the hypocrisy of her professional pose became increasingly painful and was undoubtedly one reason why she left a career in journalism for the orange grove at Cross Creek. She dryly remarked years later that the money she made by writing "Songs of the Housewife" may have enabled her to avoid one kind of prostitution but not another.

During these newspaper years she also wrote short fiction continuously, trying with growing despair to discover those elements of popular taste which she felt must be satisfied in order for her to write stories that would sell. It was the wrong approach. She was unable to place a single story, and she began to question seriously an assumption she had made since she was a little girl that she was destined to achieve fame as a writer. The dissatisfaction she felt with life in the city and with her work was compounded by an awareness that the marriage to Charles Rawlings was not working out and was involving them both in a constant and growing strain.

Reasons of this sort and not mere impulse sent Marjorie to Florida. Like the forty-niners she seized a chance to make a clean break with the past, to leave behind the irritations of city, job, and unhappy marriage, thinking that on the land under the bright sun perhaps she and Charles could make both marriage and writing come right. As for their fortune, if they could not make it with their typewriters, then perhaps they would find it hanging from trees planted in symmetrical, green rows.

With a big-city flourish, like someone naming a weekend cottage on a lake, they called the place "Los Hermanos" ["The Brothers"], because Charles' two brothers at first enthusiastically joined them in working the place. But life at "Los Hermanos" in those early years turned out to be no pastoral idyll. All four worked hard tending the grove, planting crops of string beans, milking cows, mending the fences, but with all their labor things got tighter and tighter. There were freezes and droughts, heavy wet spells, windstorms, and the terrible threat of the Mediterranean fruit fly which had infested the lower part of the state and was slowly moving northward. Fertilizer, spray, seed, and machinery made disastrous inroads on the meager cash reserves. Within two years both Wray and James Rawlings had given up the struggle and had returned North to less heartbreaking work. But both Marjorie and Charles had begun to write—he of the sponge fishery at Tarpon Springs, she of the country and the folk around her.

If Marjorie's coming to Cross Creek was, as she always freely admitted, a flight from the city and an attempt to find a happier life in a simpler, more elemental world, it was also a last desperate attempt to find herself as a writer. After a decade of fruitless effort, she was nearly in despair. Her true problem was that she had nothing to write about, nothing that was "real" in the sense of being a part of her own experience of life. She was like the other members of her generation whom Malcolm Cowley has described as being "deracinated" by their education. In school and in college they were taught to ignore the life around them in favor of a surface culture, mainly humanistic and related almost entirely to Europe and the past, a culture which one could put on like a British suit or an Oxford accent. Literature in this context meant the writings of British or European poets and novelists, and to write literature meant to emulate them.

At Wisconsin, in the classes of William Ellery Leonard and in nightlong discussions with her colleagues on the *Lit*, Marjorie had become acquainted with the "new poetry." She had seen Vachel Lindsay in person and had written an account of his visit to the campus, but her own poems in the *Lit* were echoes of Browning, Housman, or Swinburne; her published prose pieces almost entirely fanciful or ephemeral. One of her associates on the *Lit* who later became a journalist, said of her, "She wrote verses . . . about 'Little Grey Town of Tumbledown' and other places hard to locate geographically because they existed only in her lively fancy. About real places or real people she did not write, having had little experience of them, and withdrawing, in fact, from hateful contacts with reality which might cloud the bright world of imagination where she felt more at home" [Ernest L. Meyer, in a review of *SMU*, Madison *Capitol-Times*, March 2, 1933]. During the twenties she continued to make this separation between the realms of reality and imagination, to write as if literature came only out of the imagination. As a result her stories had a disembodied air, were full of stereotyped characters, of romantic or melodramatic excesses, as if she were working with materials that were not quite real. The tragedy and color of actual life which she daily encountered as a newspaper woman never seemed the proper substance for fiction. She moved to Florida because she was convinced that a change in setting might provide a needed change in key for her writing. She meant to exchange the city for the farm, the rigor of a northern climate for the bright sunshine of the semitropics. It was only after she had lived in Florida for a time that she discovered in her "cracker" neighbors a subject matter which appealed powerfully to her imagination and allowed her romantic sensibilities fullest exercise, but which was at the same time anchored in a living reality. The result was a kind of delayed explosion.

Like a traveler making a record of a place strikingly different from the familiar world which he has left, she at first wrote down her impressions in the form of a journal or as isolated sketches or narratives, and at first the instincts of the reporter were more engaged than those of the creative artist. Like other Yankee newcomers she was continually amazed at the lavishness of the natural beauty which surrounded her. She described the plants and animals, the look of the landscape and sky, the flow of the seasons, the working of the grove and the truck crops, the war against the fruit fly, and the miseries of "red-bugs," ants, and mosquitoes. She also began to put her neighbors on record, those living close at hand in Cross Creek and Island Grove, then a widening circle of people including cracker families living in the Big Scrub. At first the quaintness of these people attracted her attention—their hard, simple life, their apparent backwardness, their picturesque ways and speech. Soon she was attracted by more than novelty. The more she knew these people, the more she loved them and the simple grace of their way of life. She was struck especially by the apparent harmony with which they lived with their wild background.

She had the sense that she was watching the American frontier past somehow come to life in a setting as exotic as that of *Green Mansions*, and she could hardly write fast enough to record what she saw before it was swept away by advancing civilization or before her own sensitivity of eye and ear grew dull from familiarity.

This pull she felt toward elemental things, which was one of the strongest forces in her mature attitude toward life, was something she shared with many other American writers of her generation. A similar fascination with the primal lies behind the pastoral art of Robert Frost, and behind a number of Faulkner's most important novels. The elemental things are what Wolfe sought behind "the unfound door," and what Hemingway looked for in the Michigan woods and in the green hills of Africa, and what he admired most in the Spanish peasants. There can be no doubt that Marjorie felt in the early 1930's, as she contemplated the world of the "crackers," that she had actually discovered Wolfe's unfound door and that through it she could step out of the modern world, back in time, back to the frontier childhood of the American people, back to the way life was before machines, before things got complicated and mixed up, back to the time when a man could enclose the basic facts of his life with his own mind and confront them with his own strength and skill. This realization was for her a true epiphany, flooding her consciousness with sudden illumination and a sense of urgency and excitement, and within two years of her arrival in Florida she had peered deeply enough into this lost world that she had set down in substance the outlines of her most important books and stories.

Most of her writings of literary value have Florida backgrounds, and most of these were produced from 1929 to 1942, with a definite peak of productivity occurring between 1937 and 1942. She sold the first piece she sent out—a gathering of sketches and local color anecdotes which she put together in 1929, scarcely a year after her arrival, to which she gave the title, "Cracker Chidlings," and started on the rounds of the major literary journals. *Scribner's* magazine bought them in

March, 1930, for $150—not a lot of money, but nevertheless a radical event in her life. She had told herself that she would no longer write with an eye on possible sales, would no longer try to produce "literature"; she would write simply and honestly of this new country and of this people she was beginning to love, and if the stories did not sell she would give up writing for good. She was later to wince at the mention of these first Florida sketches, because she came to think of them as regional studies which were more journalistic than creative; but, if they were crude compared to her later writings, they were radically different and far superior to anything she had written up to that time. They were the first of her writings to have the red blood of life, and they lived up in a measure to the claim of their subtitle, "Real tales from the Florida interior." They were real enough to gravel the editor of the Ocala, Florida, *Star*, who delivered an indignant blast on the editorial page denying that Florida crackers were anything like what Marjorie had pictured. He claimed that she must have gotten her knowledge of the southern poor-white from visiting the Cumberland mountain region, that no one in Florida either acted or talked as she had represented these people. Marjorie never took back a word, but engaged the editor in strong rebuttal, declaring that he obviously knew less about the people in his own region than she did, even if she was a Yankee newcomer. She was right, and the man backed down. She did know more, because she had set about with extraordinary energy to learn everything she could about her cracker friends, and she had the eyes of the gifted writer which missed nothing and one of the sharpest ears for human speech of any writer in her generation.

One of the most important consequences of the sale of these sketches to *Scribner's* magazine was that even before they appeared in print they caught the eye of Maxwell Perkins, the chief editor in Scribner's publishing department. The word "great" is infrequently bestowed upon editors, but Maxwell Perkins was surely one of the persons to whom it applies. He is best remembered as the man who helped Thomas Wolfe shape his wheelbarrow loads of manuscript into publishable form, and as the editor behind Scott Fitzgerald and Ernest Hemingway. He was also a major and indispensable factor in the literary career of Marjorie Kinnan Rawlings, who in a real sense was his discovery, and who, from 1930 until his death in 1947, looked to him for counsel, encouragement, and friendship. Perkins was a quiet, self-effacing man, with a New Englander's reserve, but with warmth under the reserve and a wit and sharp intelligence and sure instinct in literary matters. He had the special gift, without being in any way obtrusive or demanding, for helping his writers find the best that was in them. From their earliest exchanges of letters Marjorie had unreserved faith in his literary judgment, and such was the force of his quiet presence that she wrote always with one ear half-cocked for his approval. With the intuition which was part of his special genius, he sensed underneath "Cracker Chidlings" a potential for something much finer and sent Marjorie a pleasant note asking if she had thought of writing fiction based on these wonderful cracker people. Her reply was ebullient:

"I am vibrating with material like a hive of bees in swarm. . . . At present I see four books very definitely: two of them would take several more years of note-taking. Of the two I am about ready to begin on, one would be a novel of the scrub country [*South Moon Under*]. I managed to get lost in the scrub the first day of the hunting season—and encountered for the first time the palpability of silence. So isolated a section gives a value to the scattered inhabitants" [MKR to MEP March 31, 1931]. She was never to forget this experience, which always had mystic significance to her. Far from being frightened when she knew she was definitely lost and alone, she sat down on a log and simply waited, and a sense of peace deeper and more pervasive than anything she had ever known settled over her. She was reluctant to reply when after an hour she heard the signal shots of the rest of the party who had by now left their hunt and begun a search for her. A significant part of the experience was her sense that such a country with its wildness and its silence must have some pronounced effect upon the character of people who lived there. She was to go back later to the scrub for a longer stay to discover more about these people and their way of life.

The second book she planned at this time was a story of an Englishman exiled by his family with a remittance to Florida about the time of the Big Freeze of 1895. She meant to contrast the misery of this man who came as an outsider, hating the savagely beautiful country, with the simple beauty of the lives of native crackers, whose lives were hard but in harmony with their surroundings. This story was published as *Golden Apples* in 1935. The third book she had in mind was to be a chronicle of life at Cross Creek, a kind of biography of the place. For more than ten years she kept this project in mind, saving anecdotes and ideas, and eventually published the book as *Cross Creek* in 1942.

The fourth full-length story she intended involved a Florida Paul Bunyan named Big Bill Bell who worked as a hard-driving railroad construction foreman for the Atlantic Coast Line in the Suwannee River valley. She got as far with this story as putting together a loosely connected series of sketches based on material gathered in interviews in the Trenton area, gave these the title, "Lord Bill of the Suwannee River," and started them on the rounds of the literary magazines. *Scribner's* turned them down, as did the *Atlantic* with a brief note saying that these were very interesting but it was a pity they hadn't been worked into a real narrative. Marjorie was too engrossed with her other attempts to get this country on record to be much concerned with the rejection of one piece. She thrust "Lord Bill" into a drawer intending to come back later for a reworking, but in the meantime she turned her attention to three other pieces of short fiction. Each of these was a fictionized account of real-life people or incidents and they illustrate the manner in which she was learning to convert her experience into literature. "A Crop of Beans" was based upon the occasion when she and Charles with the help of an old Negro saved a crop of string beans from late frost in the spring of 1931 by covering over the young plants with sand until the danger had passed. They made a killing in the produce market because everyone else's beans had been frozen out. Another story called "Alligators" came from a group of tales which Marjorie had heard chiefly from her cracker neighbor, Fred Tompkins. She gave the tales unity by putting them in the mouth of a slow-talking narrator who tells the most hilarious and outrageously exaggerated events in a dead-pan manner reminiscent of Mark Twain. She finished off at once a long story called "High Winds," involving the struggle of a young cracker couple to make their living in this wild country, by trapping, fishing, and hunting. Revised in accordance with Perkins' suggestions, and renamed "Jacob's Ladder," it was bought by *Scribner's* magazine and published in the April issue of 1931.

Thus by the late spring of 1931, though she had seen only two of her pieces in print, she knew she had found her subject matter and was swiftly learning an effective technique for handling it. The thoroughness with which she attempted to penetrate to an understanding of cracker life is illustrated by her going to the Big Scrub to live for two and a half months in the late summer of this same year. She knew three of the handful of families living there and made arrangements to live chiefly with the Fiddia family—a ninety-pound white-haired wisp of a woman who still plowed her own field behind a mule, and her son Leonard, master woodsman, hunter, trapper, and fisherman, who, report had it, also had some share in a moonshine still and would be willing for Marjorie to help him operate it at night. She wrote Perkins with self-conscious bravado not to be surprised if she wrote him from jail and not to bail her out if she did because the jailhouse would be such a splendid place to write. She lived in the scrub from mid-August till the end of October, and immediately after her return to Cross Creek she began to convert her experience into fiction.

Her first account of life in the scrub was *South Moon Under* which was published by Scribner's in March of 1933, an edition appearing in England simultaneously under the Faber and Faber imprint. The critical reaction was almost unanimously enthusiastic: "a book of great distinction," "clarity of style," "fresh, honest, poetic," "rich in the humor of natural man," "pre-eminently American," "a great new talent." There was serious suggestion that the book deserved the Pulitzer prize for fiction. The Book-of-the-Month Club adopted it for their March selection, as a dual offering with George Bernard Shaw's *Adventures of a Black Girl in Her Search for God*. Marjorie's first major effort was a distinct success.

But the silver cloud of March, 1933, had its black lining. The move to Florida in 1928 had for a time eased the strain which had threatened her marriage to Charles Rawlings. The adventure of their flight from the city, the challenge of the struggle to make the orange grove pay, the outdoor life with its hunting and fishing, had all appealed to Charles as much as to her, but after five years much of the novelty had worn off, and, in spite of an occasional lift, as when they saved the bean crop from frost to make a spectacular profit, Charles had become increasingly bored with the routine of Cross Creek life. Even though the Gulf and the Atlantic Ocean were only sixty miles away, he disliked living inland and missed boats and big water. For several years his own writing had called him away for increasingly prolonged periods—to the sponge fishery at Tarpon Springs, to yachting events in the Great Lakes region or the Northeast. Their life together had less and less in common. Ironically, the success of *South Moon Under* provided the occasion for the final break.

About a month after the book was published, Perkins sent Marjorie a big manila envelope full of reviews clipped from all over the United States and England. Nearly all were full of praise for the new talent. Here was the fame for which she had yearned so long, but instead of filling her with elation, it sent her into a mood of intense melancholy; it meant nothing, it was ashes in the mouth. She looked up from the reviews with such misery that Charles asked if she wanted to be alone. She said yes. He packed and left for the seacoast, and they both understood that he was not coming back. The separation was made final by a divorce decree granted seven months later. With more years, Marjorie was to learn that her depression following *South Moon Under* was a common experience of authors after a major work; but, innocent of this knowledge in 1933, she had not learned to adjust to it. Riding on the momentum built up for the novel just completed, without allowing so much as a pause for breath, she plunged at once into the preliminaries for her next book.

Unlike *South Moon Under*, which had gone forward with steady sureness, even a kind of exhilaration, *Golden Apples* proved to be a prolonged misery of indecision, false starts, and painful revisions, which in the end produced a work she never felt right about. Part of her difficulty came from her own emotional turmoil following the break with Charles. The separation meant freedom from one kind of tension, but it left a void in her life, a restlessness and loneliness which she found difficult to cope with. She tried to ease the hurt by leaving Cross Creek temporarily and taking a long trip with her friend Dessie Smith, in a row boat powered by an outboard motor down a hundred miles of the upper St. Johns River. She later gave an account of this trip in her piece called "Hyacinth Drift." She had a bright moment when the O. Henry Memorial Prize Award committee gave its first prize of $500 to "Gal Young Un," a narrative concerning a worthy young woman of good family who married a flashy, shiftless, backwoods bootlegger. She started improvements on the house at Cross Creek with some of the royalty money now coming in from *South Moon Under*—inside plumbing to replace the outhouse, a handsome new roof of split cypress shingles to replace the unsightly sheet metal. In midsummer she made a voyage to England, telling herself it was a research trip to provide background on her Englishman in the new book.

None of these gave more than temporary respite for her troubled spirit or for the uncertainties which impeded progress on *Golden Apples*, an ill-starred book from the beginning. In this book Marjorie meant to demonstrate that she was not limited as a writer to a realistic treatment of the Florida scene, and she added to the original story, which developed a contrast between two crackers and a young Englishman in their relationship to a Florida setting, a whole new sequence concerning a wealthy foxhunting set, a kind of Florida squirearchy headed by a colorful young woman named Camilla Van Dyne. The first half of the book, which was devoted to the young crackers and to a rendering of the Florida background, was beautifully written; the second half, almost entirely a product of her own imagination, was sodden with stereotypes and melodramatic excesses like those in her unpublishable stories of the twenties. Perkins recognized the basic difficulty and urged her to simplify the story and to moderate the romantic elements, but he was engrossed with Wolfe and *Of Time and the River* and was never able to give *Golden Apples* his full attention. Marjorie squeezed out some of the flaws through several painful revisions, but not before her whole involvement with the book had become a kind of nightmare.

While she was in the midst of revision, her literary agent, Carl Brandt, sold the serial rights to the story to Hearst's *Cosmopolitan* for $1,200, which was more than Marjorie could turn down, but this forced her to drop everything and write a reduced version of the story in four installments. She had completed only two of these installments when she broke her neck in a fall from a horse and finished the rest of the work on the book with her head in a brace, which, she said ruefully, gave her a look like Joan of Arc listening for the angels. Even when the serial version was completed in April of 1935, pressure was still on for revision of the full-length version to meet an August publishing schedule. In an agony of worry because she knew the thing was not right, in constant pain from her injury and increasing discomfort from summer heat, she plugged on with revisions through May, June, and July, and reluctantly let the book go to press in August, a two-ply, divided story, much inferior to *South Moon Under*. It had cost her two years of misery, but from it she learned lessons which made possible her two best books, which were now to follow.

The Yearling provides a good example of the manner in which Marjorie and Maxwell Perkins worked together on a book. In essence Perkins gave her the opportunity for a dialogue, chiefly by mail, in which she could clarify her thinking, test her ideas, work off moods of frustration and disgruntlement, and bring her tentative efforts for a review. He always listened with patience and a genuine sympathy, offered suggestions, and gave invaluable criticism and encouragement, but scrupulously avoided usurping any of the artist's creative function. The dialogue concerning *The Yearling* began in June, 1933, when Marjorie had bogged down trying to get *Golden Apples* moving. Sensing her frustration, he wrote asking if she had ever thought of doing a book about a child in the scrub. Marjorie was interested and in her reply told of how in Washington when she was a girl she would gather the young children of the neighborhood around her on the steps of a church in the evening and tell them stories. At this stage both he and she were thinking in terms of a juvenile—a book *for* children. For four months she said no more about it, but in October, with *Golden Apples* now hurting like a bad tooth, she wrote asking for more details about his idea of the "boy's book of the scrub," and wondering if he had not suggested it because he thought she couldn't do the novel. As always he was reassuring, and then went on to suggest that she try a book similar to *Huckleberry Finn*, *Treasure Island*, or Kipling's *Kim*, in which the heroes were boys and the stories of adventure in the out-of-doors. He suggested that she use the same kind of material which had made *South Moon Under* so attractive—river trips, dogs and guns, and hunting in the wilderness.

Marjorie was now sufficiently engaged with the idea to arrange to live once more in the scrub, this time with the family of an old hunter named Cal Long, whose father shortly after the Civil War had homesteaded a plot of ground in the scrub when it was still an unspoiled wilderness. She meant to collect information and stories from the old man about his early life as pioneer and hunter but, though he was cordial and cooperative, usable material seemed to come slowly and Marjorie was restless. After a week she returned to Cross Creek, with her mind definitely made up to put the boy's book aside for the time being and concentrate her entire effort on pushing *Golden*

Apples through to completion. It was more than two years before she returned to it.

After *Golden Apples* she turned her attention to several pieces of short fiction while the question of a longer work simmered. "The boy's book of the scrub," which had seemed so attractive two years earlier, now aroused no enthusiasm; the material seemed thin. She rewrote a story called "Ol' Mule," expanding it and giving it the new title of "Varmints" and using as narrator Quincy Dover, the fat cracker woman who first appeared in a comic story, "Benny and the Bird Dogs." The mule story went so well that she projected another Quincy Dover story based on cockfighting in the local area ["Cocks Must Crow"], and thought seriously of doing enough stories based on Quincy to fill a volume. She also revived an old intention of writing a book which would be an account of the place where she lived; she now had a title for it, *Cross Creek: A Chronicle.* But before she got any further with this project, something clicked in her mind concerning "the boy's book." It came to her all at once that this need not be a story *for* boys, but a story *about* a boy, "a brief and tragic idyll of boyhood," she wrote Perkins, "which could not help but be very beautiful." At this stage she pictured not a novel but a long story of about fifty thousand words.

Then a second thing clicked into place, one of the chief lessons of *Golden Apples*: She knew now that she wrote best when she wrote about the homely details of Florida countryside and people, that if she was ever to write literature she had to abandon Camilla Van Dyne, the claptrap of romance, and the temptation to be "arty." She was to forget this again later, but now she knew beyond doubt that the simple things that interested her most to write about were the same things that appealed most to her readers. The thought gave her an exhilarating sense of release.

To soak herself once more in the sights and smells of the scrub, she drove out to "Pat's Island," the clearing in the tall pines west of Lake George where old Cal Long had lived. Baxter's clearing in the book was suggested by this place. In the two years since her last visit, the old hunter had died and his house, now abandoned, had begun to cave in. She walked the half-obliterated path from the house to the limestone sink nearby, thinking how the great funnel-shaped hole in the earth, deep enough for tall trees to grow below ground level on its sides, would have meant something fascinating to a boy. She was moved again by the isolation and the palpable silence of the scrub. The nearest human beings were a moonshiner four miles away in one direction, some hunters in a lodge four miles away in another direction, and no one else for nearly twenty miles. The place had an extraordinary pull on her imagination, so much so that the first title she thought of giving the book was *Sinkhole;* the second was *Juniper Creek,* after the small river which flowed through the scrub nearby. It was not until she was well into the first draft of the story that *The Yearling* occurred to her as a title, a phrase connected with the boy and the deer rather than with place.

For six months she mulled over her sheaf of notes and let the story simmer while she worked on the other things. Then in July of 1936 by good fortune she was introduced to Barney Dillard, another old-time hunter of the same generation as Cal Long, who had lived a similar life in the primitive scrub. Barney was full of hunting stories and lore of the wilderness, and talked gladly with Marjorie for days on end and, perhaps best of all, he took her out on several real bear hunts in the scrub. The more material she gathered, the more her enthusiasm for "the boy's book" grew; she felt none of the torment and uncertainty which had beset *Golden Apples.* In early September with bulging notebooks and high spirits, she rented a cottage in the mountains near Banner Elk, North Carolina, in order to be away from the late summer heat and the distraction of grove and friends at Cross Creek. Working with a sketch showing the area in the scrub where the story would take place, the location of the house and barn, of fields and woods, she started writing with complete confidence, going slowly but with steady progress into a book which she could already visualize in great detail. She returned to the Creek in late November, and for the next twelve months worked without hurry, determined this time to let nothing keep this novel from being as she wanted it—another valuable lesson from *Golden Apples.* Unlike the previous book, which had required several stages of radical rewriting, this book seemed to require little more than bluepenciling for style, the chief problem being to get rid of an occasional softness, where the idyllic tone she sought spilled over into the sentimental. By the first week of December in 1937, she was done and the manuscript went off to Scribner's.

Perkins' reaction to the book is interesting. He had liked everything Marjorie had told him about it as well as the glimpse she had given him of the first draft six months earlier. Now that he had read the completed manuscript he liked it even more and sent Marjorie a warm letter of compliment, telling her he was commissioning Edward Shenton to do drawings for the book and ordering a larger format than usual to lend it distinction. The tone of his letter suggests that at this point he thought of *The Yearling* as a better-than-average novel, but did not as yet suspect that he was dealing with a publishing bonanza or a literary classic. Within a month, as he worked with it, the book began to take hold of him. Near the end of January at the close of a letter devoted to routine publishing matters he scribbled in longhand: "I'll tell you what *The Yearling* has done for me. You know how much there is to worry about when one goes to bed these nights. [He was particularly worried about the war building up in Europe.] But my mind often goes to *The Yearling*—the country, people, and hunts—and then all is good and happy. Now that's a test of how good a book is" [MEP to MKR January 28, 1938]. These remarks by Perkins were the first riffle of applause which became a prolonged and resounding ovation for the book. The Book-of-the-Month Club chose *The Yearling* for their March selection; Carl Brandt sold movie rights to MGM for $30,000 in April; the book went to the top of the bestseller lists, where it remained for months; and Marjorie Kinnan Rawlings began to be a national celebrity.

2

The Crest of the Hill and Beyond

THE NEXT FOUR YEARS represent a peak period in Marjorie's life, not only in terms of popular success, but in terms of writing creativity and personal happiness as well. For the first time she was financially secure, even moderately wealthy. The thirties for the most part had been a lean time, with long spells when she had literally not been able to see where the next month's groceries or the next payment on the mortgage would come from. The grove made money for the first three years, but thereafter barely managed to pay its way or actually lost money. She liked to tell the story of how she was down to a box of crackers and a can of tomato soup in 1933 when the mail carrier brought her quite unexpectedly the $500 check from the O. Henry Memorial Award. The actual physical labor involved in keeping the grove going—especially after the divorce when she was alone at the Creek—was sometimes almost more than she could bear. Hiring and supervising the necessary help for house and grove, even when she could afford it, was another responsibility which made a heavy demand on her energy, but after spring of 1938 she had the heady satisfactions of great success and the relief which money could bring to material problems. In 1939 came the Pulitzer Prize and election to the National Academy of Arts and Letters, then quickly other signs of recognition: She began to know personally many of the major literary figures in the country; the national magazines were eager to publish almost anything she wrote; she had more invitations to lecture than she had time or desire to fill.

Marjorie actively disliked big cities except for brief visits, so that she was not often in metropolitan places where she might meet the other, more famous authors working with Max Perkins. Yet, in spite of her self-imposed isolation at Cross Creek, she met within a few months during 1936-37 Hemingway, Fitzgerald, and Wolfe, two of them in out of the way places. Hemingway she met in Bimini in the Bahamas while she was cruising as a guest on the yacht of a Mrs. Oliver Grinnell and shortly afterward wrote the following letter to Perkins:

Hawthorne, Florida
June 18

Dear Max:

I've had an unbelievably good time. It was somehow without reality. Even while I was being terribly happy, it seemed to be someone else who was being gay. I could live that sporting life forever, and love it, but I should never touch paper if I did it. My friend Robert Herrick—who, by the way, is desperately ill—once told me that if I were happy, the chances were that I shouldn't write. But why should torment be a pre-requisite? I find that Malvina Hoffman first called her group "The Sacrifice," by the title "Sorrow is the Mother of Beauty." I can't quite accede to this. The exquisite sensitiveness which makes sorrow strike deep is of course necessary. Otherwise, I agree with Masefield when he says "The days that make us happy, make us wise."

I was glad to meet Hemingway, and wished we could have had time for more than a brief talk. My hostess, Mrs. Oliver

Grinnell, was the former president of the Salt Water Anglers of America, and she still works with people like Zane Grey and Hemingway on conservation. He came to call on her on her yacht, and she was privately furious that he talked far more about literary things than fishing! The man astonished me. I should have known, from your affection for him, that he was not a fire-spitting ogre, but I'd heard so many tales in Bimini of his going around knocking people down, that I half-expected him to announce in a loud voice that he never accepted introductions to female novelists. Instead, a most lovable, nervous and sensitive person took my hand in a big gentle paw and remarked that he was a great admirer of my work. He is immensely popular with the anglers, and the natives adore him. The day before I left, he battled six hours and fifty minutes with a 514-lb. tuna, and when his "Pilar" came into harbor at 9:30 at night, the whole population turned out to see his fish and hear his story. There was such a mob on the rotten dock that a post gave way, and his Cuban mate was precipitated into Bimini Bay, coming to the surface with a profanity that was intelligible even to one who speaks no Spanish. A fatuous old man with a new yacht and a young bride had arrived not long previously, announcing that tuna fishing, of whose difficulties he has heard, was easy. So as the "Pilar" was made fast, Hemingway came swimming up from below-decks, gloriously drunk, roaring, "Where's the son of a bitch who said it was easy?" The last anyone saw of him that night, he was standing alone on the dock where his giant tuna hung from the stays—using it for a punching bag.

A story, told and re-told in Bimini, is of Hemingway's knocking down a man named Platt, for calling him a big fat slob. "You can call me a slob," Hemingway said, "but you can't call me a big fat slob," and he laid him out. Now the natives have a song which they will sing to you if they are sure Hemingway isn't about—"The big fat slob's in the harbor."

There is, obviously, some inner conflict in Hemingway which makes him go about his work with a chip on his shoulder, and which makes him want to knock people down. He is so great an artist that he does not need to be ever on the defensive. He is so vast, so virile, that he does not need ever to hit anybody. Yet he is constantly defending something that he, at least, must consider vulnerable. It seems to me that there is a clue to it in the conflict between the sporting life and the literary life; between sporting people and the artist. That life on the water, with its excitement, which almost nothing that I have experienced can equal, is a self-containing entity. When you are a part of it, nothing else seems valid. Yet occasionally a knife would go through me, and I became conscious of treachery to my own, and when I put it behind me, I felt a great guilt. The sporting people are delightful. They lave your soul. You feel clean and natural when you are with them. Then when you leave them, you are overcome with the knowledge that you are worlds away from them. You know things they will never know. Yet they wear an armor that is denied you. They are somehow blunted. It is not so much their money, for some of them are not unduly prosperous, but their reaction to living. They enjoy life hugely, yet they are not sensitive to it.

Hemingway is among these people a great deal, and they like and admire him—his personality, his sporting prowess, and his literary prestige. It seems to me that unconsciously he must value their opinion. He must be afraid of laying bare before them the agony that tears the artist. He must be afraid of lifting before them the curtain that veils the beauty that should be exposed only to reverent eyes. So, as in "Death in the Afternoon," he writes beautifully, and then immediately turns it off with a flippant comment, or a deliberate obscenity. His sporting friends would not understand the beauty. They would roar with delight at the flippancy. They are the only people who would be pleased by the things in his work that distress all the rest of us. He injects those painfully foreign elements, not as an artist, but as a sportsman, and a sportsman of a particular type.

Bimini caught at my throat the way the scrub does. The struggle there for existence is terrific. Last summer's hurricane swept it almost bare—most of the roofs, most of the cocoanut palms, the shrubs. Typhoid and malaria followed. A little white girl who followed me like a dog one morning when I got up before dawn to walk along the high crest of the island, told me that her whole family except herself and her mother had been wiped out by the fever. A six-foot West Indian nigger with a beautiful, tender face who caught our bonefish bait for us, had not tasted meat for a year and a half. There are about five hun-

dred blacks, and some thirty or forty whites. The whites, I think, are all a bit batty. There is a nightmare quality about their lives. And the beauty of the water about them is incredible. The color close to the island, in full sunlight, is the palest jade-green. At a little distance, it is aquamarine. Across the horizon, it deepens into a purple for which I know no name. And when you are out on the deep water, it is the purest indigo. Unless someone really good, like Hemingway, does something about it, I'd like to go and live there a while some day. There is a stirring novel there. I can see its outlines and most of its people, very plainly. . . .

I couldn't have liked anyone as much as I liked Hemingway, without his liking me a little. So perhaps now he and his family will stop off with me some time on one of those long drives—I am most conveniently located for it—and perhaps you would be willing to come too, then, and see my part of Florida. . . .

Always my best,
Marjorie

Soon after this she wrote to Hemingway, inviting him to make Cross Creek a stopover for his family on their way to and from Key West, and asked him if there was any way to persuade Max Perkins to visit her in Florida. Perkins steadfastly refused her invitations, but she was convinced that he would love the country which he knew so well from her books and letters, and in any case she wanted the pleasure of showing it to him and of having the chance to entertain him at Cross Creek. Hemingway wrote a friendly reply, saying that he would love to stop at the Creek sometime and possibly take in some of the turkey shooting she had offered to show him, but declined any interest in the bear hunting she mentioned. He said that he was corrupted now and liked to shoot only animals that ran both ways, but would shoot anything that flew in any direction, especially turkey. Marjorie also had mentioned in her letter her theory about the conflict in him between the sportsman and the artist. He answered that he had always fished and hunted since he could carry a cane pole because of the inner pleasure it gave him, that he had been writing for a shorter time, but it gave him the same kind of pleasure. The writing was harder to do, and he thought that sometimes he would go crazy with the difficulty and the times when you couldn't do it, if he wasn't able to mix the writing with the hunting and fishing and drinking. He agreed that the sporting crowd were "awfully dumb" but he liked them and got along all right with them. He thought Max Perkins was shy of going to Cross Creek for a visit simply because Marjorie was an unmarried woman, but promised to do what he could to persuade him to make a visit.

The visits never materialized—either from Hemingway or Perkins. Not long after this, Hemingway went off to Spain and by the time he returned to the States the brief contact with Marjorie had lapsed. They met only once more, years later, by accident in the restaurant at Marineland not far from Marjorie's beach cottage. Marjorie was entertaining Julia Scribner, the daughter of her publisher, and noticed Hemingway at another table. She sent a note over inviting him and his wife (Martha Gellhorn) to come up to her cottage for drinks. They accepted and spent a long evening there before continuing on their way West.

Marjorie's meeting with Fitzgerald was extraordinary. In September of 1936 while she was in the North Carolina mountains working on *The Yearling*, Perkins wrote her asking if she would be willing to call on Fitzgerald, who was staying at the Grove Park Inn at Asheville, recovering from a broken shoulder, from alcohol, and trying in general to pull himself together to begin another major fiction. She was willing, but quizzical, uncertain as to what good there could possibly be in the interview. Having recently read "The Crack-Up" in *Esquire*, and the lurid front-page feature by Michael Mok in the New York *Post*, which described Fitzgerald as a shaking, jittery wreck on the verge of suicide, she had an exaggerated idea of his condition, and was none too anxious to become involved. Nevertheless, she wrote to him saying that she had an errand at the pottery near Asheville and that at Perkins' suggestion she would like to call on him. He replied that he was not well but that, if she would telephone when she got into Asheville, he would be willing to see her, and suggested Friday evening, October 23. The rest of the account is in her own words and is given in some detail not only because it contains fascinating glimpses of Fitzgerald and Hemingway but because it everywhere reflects Marjorie's own warm and vivid personality and illustrates her gift for sharp observation and reportage:*

I went to the Grove Park Inn, Victorian, stuffy, overpoweringly moneyed—it had been part of Max' feeling that a writer who was working in a cabin had something to give a writer who was working in the Grove Park Inn—and when the protective manager had called up to make sure I was expected, I was taken to Scott's room. His nurse opened the door and welcomed me with icicles dripping from her starched white cap. Scott took both my hands and introduced her with a proprietary air, and her annoyance as he dismissed her for the rest of the day indicated either that she sensed I would be a bad influence for a sick patient, or that she was for the moment his mistress and resented any possible rival. I think she was probably a good nurse and not an inamorata, or he would have told me about it. He had less reticence than anyone I have ever known. It was stupid of me to have any complex about him, when he had a complex about almost everything. He began talking eagerly, saying that the last nurse had left because they had become intimate and she was terrified of becoming pregnant, and that the present nurse was devoting herself to keeping him from drinking and from other malevolent influences.

We talked at once, of course, about Max, and Scott professed to be annoyed by Max' maternalism, though I do not think he guessed why I was there. He was overwhelmingly attractive, but I was relieved to find that in spite of it, I should never have yearned for him, even in my most troubled days. He phoned down for a bottle of sherry, of a certain vintage, and he was like a little boy stealing cookies, for it seemed that liquor of any

*The Rawlings Collection in the University of Florida Library contains three manuscript accounts of this meeting: (a) a prose sketch entitled "Scott," written probably in 1948; (b) a letter to Perkins written the day after the meeting; (c) a letter to Arthur Mizener, March 18, 1948. The account given here has been arrived at by conflation, in which the three accounts have been "harmonized" so as to give a single connected version containing all essential material but avoiding duplications.

sort was forbidden. He was proud of keeping to the letter of his contract with nurse and doctor by not ordering something stronger. He could as well have asked for the luncheon menu at the same time, but he phoned for that only a little later. Service delighted him.

The menu was lavish, and he ordered lavishly, scarcely consulting me. He talked like a machine gun, mostly about himself, and I was glad to listen. His reaction to the N. Y. Post *story had been to go to New York and kill . . . Mok, until he decided that would be a silly gesture with one arm disabled. He was terribly hurt about it, of course, for he had listened to a sob story from Mok to let him in at all, and had responded to a lot of things the man told him—possibly spurious—about his own maladjusted wife, by talking more freely than he should have done. But he has taken the thing very gracefully and is not unduly bitter or upset about it. He was also more forgiving and reasonable than I think I should have been, about Hemingway's unnecessary crack at him in "The Snows of Kilimanjaro." We agreed that it was part of Hemingway's own sadistic maladjustment, which makes him go around knocking people down. Scott said that Hemingway had written him very violently, damning him for his revealing self-searchings in "Esquire," and Scott expressed the idea that it was just as legitimate to get one's grievances against life off the chest that way, as by giving an uppercut to some harmless weakling. He resented Hemingway's calling him "ruined," and from other things he said, it was plain to me that he does not consider himself "ruined," by a long shot.*

With luncheon, we had a dry white wine and after, he phoned for a bottle of port, and as the afternoon wore on, another and another. We might as well have had Martinis to begin with and been done with it. . . . His arm was in a sling, or cast, and there was a contraption over his bed—close beside the nurse's bed, like domestic twins—for traction and elevation of the shoulder. I asked him how he had managed "love" under those conditions, and he said that anything was possible. Then I remarked that it had always puzzled me how the hero in Hemingway's "Farewell to Arms" had managed intercourse with his beloved, with a broken leg. He lifted his blond eyebrows and said again that anything could be arranged when the desire was strong.

He was exhilarated. He talked of his own work. He was

modest, but he was sure. *He said that he had made an ass of himself, that his broken bone was the result of his having tried to "show off" in front of "debutantes" when he dived proudly into a swimming-pool, that he had gone astray with his writing, but was ready to go back to it in full force.*

He talked a great deal about Hemingway. He told me most intimate details. Hemingway, he said, had had his testicles shot off in the first World War, in Italy, and an Italian surgeon had grafted on a new set. "It must have worked," Scott said, "because he had children after that. But I think it made him feel he had to prove his manhood. Later, in Paris, he boasted about sleeping with a prostitute six days a week, and with his wife the seventh. I think it has influenced all his writings. In "The Sun Also Rises," the hero had exactly the same accident, but didn't come out of it as Hemingway did. A writer always takes revenge on his characters."

He said among many other things, that Ernest had written much as he did, because he couldn't play football. He talked of the caste system at such places as Princeton and Harvard, and I realized that a great part of Scott's writings and personal difficulties came from a sense of insecurity, of inferiority in the face of such a collegiate system. My impression of him was of the true artist, who had been conditioned to false values, and that while he understood that the values were spurious, could not disassociate himself from them.

I am firmly convinced that the man is all right. I know just what his state of mind has been. The same kind of panic hits anyone like me, with no one dependent on me. With an ill and expensive wife, a child brought up to luxury, and then one thing after another going wrong—"the times," as Hemingway wrote me, "when you can't do it"—it was natural enough for him to go into a very black mood. It lasted longer and he publicized it more than most of us—I am always ashamed to let anyone know about mine—but I should lay a heavy wager that he's safely on the way out.

We disagreed heartily about many things, of course. Principally as to what we expect of life. I expect the crest of the wave to have a consequent and inevitable trough, and whenever I'm at the bottom, I know there will be an upturn sooner or later. Then when I'm at the top, I don't expect it to last indefinitely—

he said that he did!—but know there will have to be less pleasant things coming along sooner or later.

He said, "You're not as much of an egotist as I am." Then he said and more or less correctly, too, that a writer almost had to be an egotist, to the point of megalomania, because everything was filtered through his own universe.

His point of view lets him in for much desperate unhappiness and disillusion, because he simply cannot expect the consistent perfection and magnificence of life that he does, frankly, expect. But as a writer, except for the times such as this one has been, when his misery holds him up too long, his masochism will not interfere with his work. We talked from a little after one, until five-thirty, when his nurse came back and fussed about his not resting, but we never reached talk of our plans for the future in any detail. He did say that he had a plan—and he spoke with every sign of the secret pleasure that is an indication of work in the brewing.*

He spoke of the autobiographical thing, but said he could not do it with most of the people alive. That he could only do it now in a pleasant way, and it wouldn't be any fun without a little malice. . . .

I feel I had no tangible help for him—he is in no truly desperate need of help—and our points of view are very different—but there is a most helpful stimulation in talk between two people who are trying to do something of the same thing—a stimulation I miss and do not have enough of, at Cross Creek. And I am sure that stimulation was good for him.

I remember being impressed by the affection with which he spoke of Hemingway and of two or three other writers—I forget who they were. He also spoke of Hemingway with a quality that puzzled me. It was not envy of the work or the man, it was not malice. I identified it as irony. It is of course the most valuable quality in his writing. At times he turned this irony on himself, quickly, and away again, as though he swung a flashlight on a dark thicket into which he had no intention of penetrating deeply. This was not for cowardice, I felt, but as though

* In this account from the letter to Perkins, she plays down the length of time they talked and the amount they drank. Both other accounts suggest that they talked until fairly late in the evening.

he intimated that it was enough for one to know the darkness was there.

He was looking very well at this time. He was not interested in me as a writer or as a woman, but he turned on his charm as deliberately as a watertap, taking obvious pleasure in it. The irony was here, too, as though he said, "This is my little trick. It is my defiance, my challenge to criticism, to being shut out."

The quantities of wine had little apparent effect on him. He maintained a consistent animation for the eight hours, as I remember, that we talked, and effortlessly. I think he was anxious for me to report to Max Perkins that he was truly himself. There was also the excitement and satisfaction of an interested audience, not to "show off," but because he had been too long without mental stimulation. I kept suggesting that I must be tiring him, that I must leave, and he insisted frantically, "No, no. You can't go yet."

I said that someone had borrowed and not returned my copy of "The Great Gatsby," my favorite of his books, but I meant to get another copy and read it again. He dashed to a cupboard and from a box of books brought out a new copy for me. I asked him to sign it for me.

He said, "No, no, that won't do at all. I'll sign a copy of our luncheon menu and paste it in the book. I'll check the dishes we had."

I was both touched and embarrassed. The idea seemed so "collegiate," like marking a Prom program. Yet it was a boyish thing, naïve and eager, and it seemed to me that the adult artist was bound irrevocably to the college lad who had never felt quite secure. Now the successful man of letters was in a position to tie the two together, as a favor for me. I should have allowed him to "check the dishes," but I said that there was no need, I should remember. I looked at the menu, pasted in "The Great Gatsby," not long ago, and of course had no memory of what we had eaten.

So certainly I can report that the contact was very pleasant. And I do not think you need to worry about him, physically or psychologically. He has thrown himself on the floor and shrieked himself black in the face and pounded his heels—as lots of us do in one way or another—but when it's over, he'll go back to his building blocks again. Have you ever felt what I call the cosmic despair? It's no joke. And if you slip a little too deep in it, as he did, it's one devilish job getting out again. But he's well on the way out and I think deserves lots of credit for getting himself so well in hand again. There will perhaps be relapses, but I don't think he feels the abyss so inescapably under him.

Scott's wine had had a devastating effect on me, and in the night I found myself half-way up the highest mountain in North Carolina, quite off my path home to my cabin. The next day I re-read "The Great Gatsby," and was again overcome by its high quality. I wrote Scott with inordinate enthusiasm, and had no answer.

Some time later I was with Maxwell Perkins in New York, and mentioned that my contact with Scott had ended with what was perhaps too lyric a letter.

Max smiled his wry smile, and said shyly, "Of course, Scott thinks that all women are in love with him."

I was offended at the moment, but have come to understand that this, too, was one of Scott's defenses. . . .

Marjorie met Thomas Wolfe about nine months later when she took a draft of *The Yearling* to New York for Perkins to look over. She had admired Wolfe's work for a number of years and on several occasions had written to Perkins that she thought him one of the most gifted writers in America but that he ought to discipline himself against purple prose. Thinking that Wolfe could profit from both the fervent praise and the suggestion of more discipline, Perkins had once or twice shown him these letters and now, since his two writers were to be in the city at the same time, he thought this a good time for them to become acquainted and invited them to join him at the Chatham Walk for a drink. Wolfe started out in a taciturn mood, but grew more expansive as the afternoon wore on into evening. At nine-thirty, now feeling quite high from their drinks, they went out and ate an enormous steak dinner. Then there were more drinks and at midnight another full meal for Wolfe in a Chinese restaurant. Marjorie had always found excitement in suicide as an abstract question for discussion and broached the topic to Wolfe while he was waiting for his food. He somehow got the notion that she was urging him to go out and commit suicide, and at the top of his lungs refused to do it, "even [with a look at Perkins] to satisfy my publishers!" Marjorie began to wish she had chosen something simple like transcendentalism to discuss. At three in the morning, Wolfe insisted that they all go down to the Fulton Street fish market for oysters on the half-shell, and strode up and down the aisles flinging his arms in great gestures exclaiming at the color and beauty of the fish ranged in ice along the counters. At four he was outside again in a drizzling rain plowing his way among the vegetables in the wholesale market, Marjorie and Perkins following, as she later wrote, "like pieces broken off from a meteor in transit" [MKR to MEP n.d. (July ?), 1937]. Finally, about four-thirty, since it was too late for Marjorie to go out to Long Island where she was staying, Perkins took her along to his own house where the next morning he had to explain her to his wife and daughters. Wolfe meanwhile had called up Marjorie's hostess out on Long Island to tell her not to worry, that Marjorie was spending the night with Maxwell Perkins. After this single night in Wolfe's company, Marjorie understood better the Rabelaisian profuseness of his prose and marveled at the patience Perkins showed in working with him.

She began what was to be a lifelong friendship with Robert Frost during the winter of 1937-38, when Frost was living in Gainesville only twenty miles from Cross Creek. When he later bought a winter home in Miami Springs and for many years made a stopover in Gainesville to lecture at the University of Florida on his way North in the spring, his visit often included a run out to the Creek to see Marjorie. He particularly liked her story "Benny and the Bird Dogs" because it was a "man's kind of humor," and told her that he sometimes cornered people to read it aloud to them.

In the years following *The Yearling's* great vogue, the pine floors of the shabby farmhouse at Cross Creek were scuffed by many a famous foot—Wendell Willkie, Sigrid Undset, Wallace Stevens, Margaret Mitchell, James Branch Cabell, A. J. Cronin, Dylan Thomas. Marjorie also found herself wined and dined by the great, including luncheon at the White House with Eleanor Roosevelt, who accepted Marjorie's offer of the cottage at Crescent Beach for a respite from the frantic pace in Washington, only to be forced to change her plans at the last minute.

Marjorie had for many years admired the books of Ellen Glasgow and in 1939 she began a limited but unusually poignant friendship when she called on Miss Glasgow in Richmond while on the way to Washington. It was a pleasant meeting and apparently sank deep into Marjorie's consciousness, for more than a year later she wrote Miss Glasgow the following letter:

Crescent Beach
RFD St. Augustine
July 19, 1941

My very dear Ellen Glasgow:

I had such a vivid dream about you last night, that I must write you—which I have been meaning to do ever since our delightful brief visit together. The reality of a dream can never be conveyed to another, but you came to live with me. I was away when you came, and on my return, to one of those strange mansions that are part of the substance of dreams, you were outside in the bitter cold, cutting away ice from the roadway and piling it in geometric patterns. I was alarmed, remembering your heart trouble, and led you inside the mansion and brought you a cup of hot coffee. You had on blue silk gloves, and I laid my hand over yours, and was amazed, for my own hand is small, to have yours fit inside mine, much smaller. You chose your room and suggested draperies to supplement a valance. The valance was red chintz and you showed me a sample of a heavy red brocade of the same shade. I told you that from now on I should take care of you, and you must not do strenuous things, such as cutting the ice in the roadway. James Cabell came into the room and asked what the two of us were up to. (As of course he would!)

My memory of my time with you is quite as vivid as the night's dream. I have thought of you oftener than I can tell you. So often a personality is detached from writings, and the two in fact seem to have nothing to do with each other. You as a person have the vitality, the wit and the irony of your work, but I was not prepared to find you so warm and so beautiful, in spite of the devotion of your friends, which would indicate those things in you. . . .

With much affection,
Marjorie

Miss Glasgow replied within a week, saying that Marjorie's letter had brought her a thrilling sense of friendship and sympathy, and that since their meeting Marjorie had often been in her thoughts. Their friendship was to continue until Miss Glasgow's death in 1945 chiefly through an exchange of letters and through mutual acquaintance with James Branch Cabell. Years later it was to be the main cause for Marjorie's undertaking a biography of Ellen Glasgow.

In spite of all the publicity over *The Yearling*, Marjorie stayed on quietly at the Creek and pushed forward the writing with little break. Probably influenced by the extraordinary success of Caldwell's *Tobacco Road* on Broadway, she began a dramatized version of *South Moon Under* and, in accordance with the usual policy at Scribner's of following a major piece of fiction with a collection of short stories, she began the editing which led to *When the Whippoorwill* in 1940. She was also reading Florida history of the period of 1790 to 1840 as research for her next major book. A lawyer friend in Jacksonville had interested her in the story of the remarkable Zephaniah Kingsley, a strong-minded planter and slave trader who lived on Fort George's Island in the mouth of the St. Johns River in the early nineteenth century. This man had taken as his legal wife a full blooded African princess and attempted to ensure her right, and the right of their four mulatto children, to inherit his extensive property at his death. The preamble to his will, dated July 20, 1843, and probated in Duval County, gives an idea of what attracted Marjorie to him as subject for a book: "Whereas I am of sound mind and disposing memory and know what I'm doing, and whereas I know perfectly well that it is against the laws and conventions of life to marry a colored person, and whereas this is my property and it is not anybody's damn business what

I do with it. . . . And whereas I have an African wife, who is one of the finest women I have ever known and who has been true and faithful to me, and whereas I believe that the amalgamation of the white and colored races to be in the best interest of America, and whereas I know that what I am about to do is going to bring down on me tremendous criticism, but I don't give a damn. Now therefore I give my wife. . . ." He then bequeathed the major portion of his estate to his wife, Anna Madgigaine Jai, and their children—to no effect since the will was subsequently broken by collateral white relatives. Marjorie was skittish about miscegenation as a theme, but was fascinated by the fictional possibilities of such a man. Before she had a chance to pursue this intention very far, she was forced by a crisis in health to set all her writing aside.

For years she had been troubled by sudden, intense, abdominal pains, had undergone an appendectomy in 1931 for relief only to discover that her appendix had been perfectly healthy, and therefore not the cause of the trouble. Now she had another severe attack and was advised by a surgeon friend in Tampa that she needed major surgery for diverticulosis—a disorder of the lower intestinal tract, the operation for which she was told had a forty per cent record of fatality. She made arrangements to be admitted to St. Joseph's Hospital in Tampa, with surgery scheduled for June 15, then wrote Perkins a *morituri te salutamus* letter, in which she tried in a melodramatic situation to be as matter-of-fact as possible. She named her brother Arthur as her executor, and said that her affairs in Florida would be in the hands of her good friend, Norton Baskin. She told Max how much she had always valued his friendship and then bade him a kind of tentative, final farewell. Perkins was shaken by the obvious gravity of Marjorie's situation and immediately sent a note to her expressing deepest concern and another to Norton Baskin asking to be informed of developments at the earliest possible moment. He received a telegram two days later advising that the operation had been called off. Mr. Baskin and two close friends had talked Marjorie into consulting Dr. T. Z. Cason at the Riverside Hospital in Jacksonville for a confirming diagnosis before submitting to surgery. His examination revealed the same disorder, but he strenuously advised against surgery except as a last resort and urged that she first try rest and a strict diet. With a definite sense of reprieve and convinced that she had had a close brush with the death angel, Marjorie settled back, not unwillingly, for a time of laziness and being cared for. "The chances are," Dr. Cason told her, "if you had gone through with that operation, you'd be cavorting with the angels about now." Marjorie put her three friends on notice that since they had saved her life they were responsible for her happiness and not to be surprised to get a call in the middle of the night saying, "I'm unhappy, come at once and cheer me up."

It was to be a year and a half before she felt able to return to sustained effort on a major book, an interim filled with several pieces of short fiction and various kinds of busy work. Her one major regret about the future when she thought she might not live had been that she would not be able to do the long-intended book about Cross Creek. Finally in February of 1940, having abandoned the Kingsley project and the intended dramatic version of *South Moon Under*, when the galleys for *When the Whippoorwill* had been sent in, she turned her full energy to *Cross Creek*. From the first it was an unusual book. It was not strictly autobiographical, though Marjorie and her life at the Creek for thirteen years were central to it; it was not topographical, simply about a place, though the little community and the country round about were also central to it. It was both narrative in part and essay in part; it contained both light, comic passages and serious, reflective passages; it was realistic, using real names and true events, yet it also had an idyllic cast. It was as much a labor of love as anything she ever wrote, and yet she went through agonies trying to find a structural scheme and a tone which would hold such diverse elements together. It took nearly two years of intense effort and four versions before she had something she was satisfied with—and she had started out with drafts or sketches of most of the book's content, material she had been saving over a ten-year period.

In this book as in *The Yearling* she profited greatly from the dialogue with Perkins (it was he, for example, who suggested a way of solving the problem of structure). Toward the end of the long process, she began to feel uneasy about having used the true names of her Cross Creek neighbors and asked for his reaction to the possibility of libel. Normally astute and hard-headed on the practical matters of publishing, Perkins was too relaxed on this occasion. His letters suggest that he was beguiled by the warmth and charm of the book, and possibly by his own knowledge of Marjorie's abundant good will toward people—particularly her neighbors. His first quick reaction to her question was to assure her that if the people were as she represented them, then there was no danger of libel; but then he began to have queasy second thoughts and asked her to tone down one chapter where the Alachua County court was represented in an undignified light. Essentially he threw the problem back to Marjorie with the suggestion that she make the decision since she knew the people involved better than anyone else. Both of them made the mistake of looking too much outside the book rather than to the statement of the book for an answer. Marjorie did check with one person who she thought might take offense and got favorable response; there was no one else she was worried about. "The negroes, Snow, Old Boss, the Glissons, the Bernie Basses, Zelma the census taker, are perfectly all right," she wrote. She was correct in all cases but one. Her misjudgment of Zelma Cason was to cost her a painful and expensive legal process which dragged on for more than five years.

The book itself, when it appeared in March of 1942, was another immediate success both with critics and public. It was once more the choice of the Book-of-the-Month Club, went into printing after printing in the regular trade edition, and was published in a special Armed Services edition and distributed to thousands of servicemen all over the world. Beyond question, Marjorie seemed now to have found the golden touch in her writing, the secret that would unlock her wordhoard. Every thing she had written since 1935 had shown the red rich glint of the true metal. There was hardly a dissenting voice among the critics praising the high literary quality of her work; she was beginning to be regarded as a major writer whose future held only promise. Equally important, her books and stories were read and loved by many thousands of readers from every walk of life; her mailbox contained almost daily spontaneous letters of praise—from a schoolboy of twelve delighted with Jody and his fawn; from a famous naturalist complimenting the accuracy and depth of her depiction of nature; from a hunting club located on Juniper Creek in the scrub praising the authenticity of her hunting sequences; from so distinguished a writer as Ellen Glasgow a note using the word "genius" in reference to *The Yearling*. Here was fulfillment of her childhood ambition for literary fame larger than she had dreamed.

With her marriage to Norton Baskin in October of 1941, she ended eight years of single life, and her personal life was now happier than it had been for many years. Her health had improved with the special diet and the operation was no longer a specter to be dreaded. The trajectory of life and career seemed to be sharply upward; from none of the visible signs was it possible to discern the curve had now reached its apogee and would begin a downward slope. One factor in the decline was the so-called "Cross Creek Trial."

Zelma Cason was one of Marjorie's oldest Florida friends, the same person who had met her at the Clyde Line dock in Jacksonville when she first arrived in Florida, the one who had first introduced her to many of the people and many of the sights in her new home. Years after the trial she claimed that she was one of two or three people that Marjorie always loved. This "friendship" was only one complicating factor in an unusually complex legal action, which began on January 8, 1943, when Zelma entered suit against Marjorie for libel, asking $100,000 damages. The nature of the suit was so ambiguous that it required eighteen months of legal maneuvering, including a decision of the Florida Supreme Court, to determine if adequate grounds for legal action existed. The state Supreme Court ruled that grounds existed if the charge was changed from libel to "invasion of privacy," and then nearly two years elapsed before the case was brought to trial in May of 1946. It was one of the most colorful cases the old red courthouse in Gainesville had ever seen. It quickly attracted wide attention from the Florida press and became one of the main events of the Gainesville social season, so that the entire action was played out before a packed house of reporters, backwoods crackers, and Gainesville housewives.

There was almost no legal precedent to guide either party in a proceeding based on "invasion of privacy," so that both sides fumbled a good deal trying to discover their most effective lines of argument, and the court at times had difficulty deciding questions of relevancy. Zelma's case was based upon the claim that several passages in *Cross Creek* had caused her great pain and humiliation, chiefly one passage from pages 48-49:

Zelma is an ageless spinster resembling an angry and efficient canary. She manages her orange grove and as much of the village and county as needs management or will submit to it. I cannot decide whether she should have been a man or a mother. She combines the more violent characteristics of both and those who ask for or accept her manifold ministrations think nothing of being cursed loudly at the very instant of being tenderly fed, clothed, nursed, or guided through their troubles.

Many persons who knew Miss Cason thought this a remarkably accurate portrait and thought it more complimentary than damaging, particularly since it was in a context almost wholly complimentary, but Zelma claimed in testimony that it had brought ridicule and abuse and had caused severe pain and embarrassment. She particularly objected to being called profane, and one of the chief issues in the trial became the nature and degree of her profaneness. The defense had some success in establishing that, though she may not have been in the habit of "taking the name of the Lord in vain," she used regularly, like many other Florida country folk, the expressions "son-of-a-bitch" and "bastard." This was all the book had said and all Marjorie had meant. In other testimony, counsel for the plaintiff sought to discredit both the book and its author by claiming that Marjorie wrote chiefly for money and that she had deliberately made the book vulgar and obscene by stressing such matters as the sex life of ducks, dogs, and pigs.

The defense tried to establish Marjorie's probity as a person and the generally high regard in which she was held by friends and neighbors by calling a large number of character witnesses, including many from Cross Creek. They tried to establish her eminence as an author by citing her accomplishments and honors; they tried to show the high regard in which the book was held by many thousands of persons over the country by citing the fact that more than five hundred thousand copies had been sold and by citing the enthusiasm of readers. They included a deputation by a navy man who said he was reading the book when his carrier the "Lexington" was torpedoed and that he stuffed the book in his pocket when he jumped overboard so he could be sure to finish reading it. They tried to establish the book's high worth as literature by calling expert witnesses, a history professor from Rollins College and the head of the English Department at the University of Florida, and by reading the deputations of persons like Henry Seidel Canby and Maxwell Perkins. They tried above all to establish the right of an author, as part of basic freedom of the press, to write the truth as he saw it.

One of the highlights of the proceeding was Marjorie's two-day testimony on the witness stand, in the course of which she showed herself a model witness, composed, astute, completely articulate, never allowing herself to become ruffled even by the most vicious personal innuendo. She told about her entire literary career, about her reasons for coming to Florida, and about her deep affection for place and people. "*Cross Creek* is a love story," she said, "of my love for the land." At one point she nearly brought proceedings to a halt when she was asked by the plaintiff's attorney to define profanity. She quietly turned the question back and asked him how he would make such a definition. He was well into a lengthy answer before being reminded by a smiling defense attorney that he didn't have to answer his own question. The spectators shouted with laughter and the judge choked as best he could behind a handkerchief while the bailiff rapped for order. During summation the already ambiguous issues were further obscured by the flowers of rhetoric which blossomed gorgeously on both sides. Counsel for plaintiff invoked the sacred honor of the Old South and Southern Womanhood, the need to beware crafty Yankee outlanders, and the right of humble country folk to be defended against the abuse of wealthy city people. Counsel for defense argued that mother would have been shocked by many expressions not considered profane by modern women; that the book should be judged by modern standards; and that the defendant was being victimized by unscrupulous lawyers eager to test a new theory in law so they could open up a new field for law cases. The judge's charge to the jury covered twelve typed pages. The jury found for the defendant in less than thirty minutes.

When the verdict was announced there was an ovation from the audience, which had been overwhelmingly favorable to Marjorie's cause throughout. But the case was not over. Zelma appealed, and for a second time the case went to the State Supreme Court, which a year later in a 3-4 decision rendered a compromise verdict, reversing the finding of the lower court but stipulating only token damages of one dollar. Marjorie was bitterly disappointed, for she saw this verdict as a defeat for an important principle; but she was advised by her attorneys that it was impossible to take the case further and settlement was finally made on August 9, 1948, more than five and one-half years after suit was begun. "It is considered by the court that the plaintiff recover of the defendants the sum of one dollar together with the costs in this behalf expended, now taxed in the sum of $1,050.10." This does not mention the more than $18,000 it cost Marjorie and her husband in legal fees.

Many things remained unsettled by this outcome. For one thing, the suit for "invasion of privacy" was little clarified; for another, Zelma's true motives were never made clear. She said in 1961 that she and Marjorie had devised the whole thing as a publicity stunt, but this seems highly unlikely when one considers the cost and the general strain and bitterness generated during the long proceedings. Some persons well acquainted with both parties have ventured the opinion that Zelma was motivated by sheer malice, by envy of Marjorie's great success, and by a desire to share some of her newly acquired wealth. Testimony during the trial asserted as much. Others feel that she started out in a mood of genuine disgruntlement at the way she had been represented in the book, meant to teach Marjorie a lesson, but fell victim to lawyers willing for their own reasons to press the case far beyond her first intention. None of this has been established as fact, and the truth may involve some combination of these conjectures or none of them.

Majorie's motives were clear from the beginning. She was puzzled at the virulence and persistence of Zelma's attack, and meant to defend herself, but more than this she was interested in defending an important principle involving the rights of authors everywhere. She was disappointed that the case had had little news coverage outside the state of Florida, and in June of 1946 following the favorable verdict of the circuit court she wrote a letter to the editor of *Time* explaining why she thought the case important: "A vital principle is involved: the right of anyone to write of his or her own life, where that necessarily involves mention of other people, short, of course, of libel. If a local jury had decided against me in this, it would seem that not only would all autobiography become immediately taboo, but that freedom of the press in its wider aspects might be curtailed. It would not be too absurd to assume, in the event of a verdict against me, that a newspaper, that *Time* magazine, would be required, at least under Florida law, to have the written permission of anyone involved in the news. . . ."

In spite of the ultimate unfavorable decision of the Supreme Court, Marjorie felt one resounding victory in the whole unpleasant business, and that was the response of her neighbors and friends. Even though she had come to Cross Creek as a Yankee outsider, while Zelma had lived in the area all her life, the people from Cross Creek and the surrounding area came swiftly and almost unanimously to Marjorie's support, so that there was no mistaking that they returned in full measure the love and esteem she held for them. Nevertheless, the trial on the whole was a bitter experience which exacted a heavy cost, not only in money, but in worry and distraction and in energy she could little spare from her writing, which after 1942 seemed to stall in spite of her determined effort to start a new book.

It is tempting to assert that there was some exhalation in the air at Cross Creek, some mystic substance in its earth which fed her creative nature, for the simple fact is that she was unable to write before she moved there and was able to write only with the greatest strain and effort after she left. Carried forward by the momentum of *Cross Creek*, she went on without pause to complete *Cross Creek Cookery* in the spring and summer of 1942, a pleasant, chatty book full of anecdotes as well as recipes, reflecting Marjorie's genius as a cook and having some of the same warmth and joy of life as the larger book from which it grew. But the publication of *Cross Creek* in early 1942 marked the virtual end of her major writing career and the end of her continuous residence at the Creek.

Just as she was finishing the final draft of the book, she married Norton Baskin and moved to St. Augustine, where her husband's business as owner and manager of the Castle Warden Hotel demanded his presence. In many ways Norton Baskin was ideally suited to be Marjorie's husband. He was a gentle, sympathetic person with great charm and social grace. He had intelligence and a natural wit as sharp as Marjorie's and real gifts as a raconteur. He had known her since the early thirties and had been a close friend and mainstay during the difficult years when she had tried to manage alone at the grove. He knew about the demands her writing made; he knew the stress that her fame would place upon the marriage, and in a quiet way he successfully resisted becoming "Mr. Marjorie Kinnan Rawlings." He did not know, and neither did she, how much the move to St. Augustine would affect the writing. While he was a pleasant companion on outdoor excursions, his own gifts were those of a city man. He loved the context of the hotel, the people, the functions, the swirl of activity, and he had a special apartment furnished for their use, a kind of penthouse at the top of the hotel, overlooking St. Augustine Bay. But as much as she desired it, Marjorie never learned to like living at the hotel. There was something too public and too citified about it. She still owned her beach cottage ten miles down the coast, to which she could get away for the quiet her work required, and Norton had a beautiful study and bath added to the cottage to make conditions as ideal as possible for her. But she never felt at rest, and always had the sense that she was only visiting and would sooner or later be going back "home" to the Creek. In the spring of 1942 she wrote to Perkins, "There is something there from which I cannot tear away. My husband is so completely lovely a person, and it grieves me to see him grieved when I simply have to clear out and go back to the Creek" [MKR to MEP March n.d., 1942]. Without being quite aware of it, she had begun to illustrate in her own life her theory that happiness and fulfillment are functions of place.

Several other things combined to make the writing more difficult. The fame which came with big success had had relatively little effect on Marjorie personally—except for occasional small bursts of arrogance and self-importance she remained her usual self—but with her writing it was a different matter. She had always felt uneasy about being labeled a regionalist, a mere "Florida" writer, and she determined now that she would show she was not chained to a single region. Having produced two books in succession which everyone told her, and which she knew herself, were really good, maybe even great, she felt under terrific pressure to do it again. The next book had to be another "big" book. Such motives as these were at work when a story began to form in her mind based on her grandfather Traphagen, who had been a farmer in southern Michigan in the decades following the Civil War. She had warm memories of the farm from summer vacations when she was a little girl, and her literary instincts now once more took her to the land and to the past. But the desire to make this book "big" led her to forget the great truth she had discovered in the pain of *Golden Apples*—that her imagination needed both the stimulus and the ballast of personal experience, and that she must write *simply* of earthy things. Once more as in the twenties she set herself to write "literature," and she felt she had to attempt major symbolism, to fill the book with ideas, to make it a searching interpretation of life. The result was her last novel, *The Sojourner*, published after a ten-year agony, in 1953, a book having many of the faults of *Golden Apples* and few of the virtues of *The Yearling*.

Before her plan for the book had fully formed, World War II broke in upon her life in radical fashion. Norton could not resist the urge to make a more direct contribution to the war effort than was possible to a St. Augustine hotel manager. In June of 1943 he volunteered as an ambulance driver in the American Field Service, was accepted, and with dramatic suddenness received his shots and his uniforms and on the second of August sailed from New York on the Liberty ship "Socotra" on the first leg of a voyage which would take him to a year's service with British troops fighting the Japanese in the wild country along the India-Burma frontier. Marjorie admired Norton for his desire to serve, but she was deeply worried about him since the troops to which he was attached were engaged in savage fighting, and she knew the casualty rate for ambulance drivers in that sector was unusually high. While he was gone she wrote him at length every day, taking hours to give him details of what was happening back home, what she was doing, what she was thinking. About this same time she became involved in a massive correspondence with other servicemen, at first answering some of the enthusiastic letters of praise for her books, but then continuing many of the exchanges thus begun, partly because she enjoyed the contact with servicemen stationed in odd places all over the world, partly as a patriotic duty.

Norton had more than his share of adventure with the American Field Service. At one time he was working with a division which was completely surrounded by enemy troops, cut off for days from the rest of the army, with no word of their fate reaching the outside. He found the precipitous mountain roads to be more harrowing than the hazards of combat itself and found himself driving in all weather and at night under blackout conditions over roads that would have been perilous in good weather and broad daylight. But within a little over a year he was back in the States, a very sick man, having been hospitalized for dysentery, and requiring weeks of rest and care before his health returned. Marjorie had pulled strings with her friends among the high brass in the Pentagon to get him space on a returning plane, then pitched into the long process of helping him back to health. They both felt lucky that he had come through without permanent injury, but the whole experience created a major lapse in her writing, a dislocation which made it almost impossible for her to get the next book started. The correspondence with servicemen she continued, but worthy as it may have been, it siphoned off literary energies she could ill spare from her serious writing.

The end of the war brought little improvement; she made half a dozen starts on the new book, but none of them was right. During the war years she had continued to write short stories and there was still power enough in her name that Carl Brandt was able to place five of these with *The New Yorker* between 1941 and 1945. All of these stories reflected her determination to efface her literary ties with the backwoods region, and in them she eschewed cracker material entirely as well as the realistic mode which went with it, trying instead for suggestive mood or for symbolic poignance. These stories all have a smooth technical finish, but only one of them, "The Pelican's Shadow," succeeds well enough to deserve a place beside her best cracker writings. The others suggest that she was trying hard but not feeling at home in the newly adopted approach to writing.

After 1945, though the Creek still tugged at her heart, she spent less and less of her time there, as the center of her life shifted gradually to St. Augustine, where her acquaintance now included a number of famous winter visitors, among them James Branch Cabell and Owen D. Young. In 1947, to help break the impasse with the writing, Mr. Young offered her the use of a cottage outside Van Hornesville, a small town in upper New York State to which he had retired after his career with

General Electric, and thus he opened a new chapter in Marjorie's life. The country around Van Hornesville was rich farm land similar to the Michigan area which was to be the setting for the new book, and Marjorie gladly accepted the offer of the cottage, thinking that the country might provide some of the stimulus she needed to get the book moving. She had barely arrived at the cottage in June when she was handed a telegram informing her that Max Perkins had died. Her first feeling was of unspeakable grief at losing the man himself, and then a feeling of frustration that she had come all the way to New York State to start a book that Max would never see and on which he could not save her from possible pitfalls. Her impulse was to return immediately to Florida and give up the whole business, but then she thought how horrified Max would be, for with him the writing had always come first. She stayed on to make another start, and the Van Hornesville area proved so appealing that in July she bought an old farmhouse facing south on a hill not far out of the village, had it remodeled, and for the next six years went there each summer to write.

From now until its end, her life can best be described as a continuous warfare in which she pitted her will to produce another major book against failing health and energy, failing literary powers, and numerous other distractions such as the Cross Creek Trial. During these last years she underwent surgery five times, as well as the shock of discovering that her eyesight was becoming affected by glaucoma. Fortunately the glaucoma could be checked by prompt treatment, but nothing could check the progressive physical decline. Many of her problems with health were caused or aggravated by the relentless way she drove herself to complete the book. One doctor described her condition by telling her that she had an engine too large for the chassis, and warned her that she would have to slow down or face the most serious kind of breakdown. She knew that he was right but the book would give her no rest. She hated to be away from Norton for long periods, and yet each summer she felt compelled to go to Van Hornesville, where she stayed on longer and longer into the fall, until she was returning

South only after snow and bitter cold made it unsafe for her to try to stay longer.

During these years she developed an accident-proneness which added to the pattern of dislocation. She was always a poor automobile driver, always drove in such a headlong fashion that it was a literally terrifying experience to ride with her. Now within a few years she had three major auto accidents, each time wrecking the car though not involving anyone in serious injury. She was troubled almost continuously by black moods of guilt and frustration which went with the slow progress in the writing. Missing the dialogue with Perkins, she turned to several other persons to fill that void—chiefly to John Hall Wheelock at Scribner's and to Norman Berg, a representative of the Macmillan Company whom she had known as a close friend for some years—but no one was able to give that almost intuitive understanding of her literary purposes that Perkins had given.

In spite of all she was fighting against, she never gave up, but clenched her teeth and persisted, and *The Sojourner* appeared finally in January of 1953. It *was* a big book in some ways, with a larger cast of characters than she had ever used before, and a generous sweep of time and space; it dealt with big themes; it was full of earthy details of Midwestern farm life in the decades following the Civil War. Yet it was one of her lesser rather than one of her greater performances, because it was flawed by romantic stereotypes and lacked the spontaneous vitality of her best Florida writings. It had a brief popular success when it was adopted by the Literary Guild and distributed to its thousands of members, but the reaction of reviewers varied from enthusiastic praise to outright panning of the book, with most critics picking a cautious way through neutral ground trying to say nice things about the book because of their respect for her previous work.

In one sense it was the most expensive book she ever wrote, since the merciless way she drove herself while writing it almost certainly contributed to her death a year after it was published. In February of 1952 she had fair warning that it was time to slow down. She was struck by a coronary heart attack one night while she was alone in the house at Cross Creek, with pain so intense that she was unable to call for help even though her Negro maid Adrenna was in the tenant house only a few hundred yards away through the grove. She had to wait all night until Adrenna came up to the house in the morning. "For all I knew," she wrote to Norman Berg, " . . . I was dying, and I have been much relieved to find that I was not at all afraid. Death seemed cold and dark and lonely, but I seemed to be looking down a straight road over-arched by trees, and the road simply went on with no end in sight, and there was no fear or dread or terror in the thought of going down it. I was interested afterward to remember I had felt this way" [MKR to NB March 2, 1952]. Even after this experience she gave herself only the briefest respite and was soon back at the manuscript, which was finished at last in the summer of 1952.

Shortly after Ellen Glasgow died in 1945, Irita Van Doren, one of her literary executors, had asked Marjorie if she would be interested in doing a biography. Still entangled in *The Sojourner*, she had said no; but when the novel was finished, she reconsidered and took on the Glasgow project as her next book, then immediately threw herself with characteristic intensity into the process of research. In the spring of 1953 she established residence in Richmond for several months so as to be able to interview surviving friends and relatives of Miss Glasgow. She had remarkable success in these endeavors, quickly gaining the confidence of a number of persons who could give her valuable first-hand information or who had important letters and papers which they opened for her use. Within a year she amassed a substantial amount of material for the book, but she never got beyond the notetaking stage. On the 14th of December in 1953 while at her home in Crescent Beach, she was struck by a cerebral hemorrhage from which she never recovered. For burial she was taken to Antioch Cemetery a few miles outside Island Grove in the midst of the Cross Creek country she had loved so well.

3

What She Was Like

Like most people, Marjorie Kinnan Rawlings was not one person but many persons. She was always conscious of deep roots in the American past since she was descended on both sides of her family from settlers who had come to the New World in the seventeenth century—Kinnans from Scotland, Pearces from England, Bogarduses from Holland. One of her early Bogardus ancestors had owned a large part of what is now Wall Street and lower Broadway, the site of present Trinity Church on Manhattan. Another of her ancestors was a Mary Kinnan, who was captured in 1791 by Shawnee Indians during a massacre in Randolph County, Virginia, and held captive near Detroit for four years. In her mother's family were Traphagens of German stock, who moved west from the Hudson Valley after the Civil War and settled in southern Michigan as independent small farmers. Marjorie was fiercely proud of her

Scottish family name, which she always pronounced Kin-nán, with strong accent on the last syllable, and she insisted that her publishers always use the full three names—Marjorie Kinnan Rawlings—as her official pen name.

The dominant impression she left on most people was of intense vitality, of a person charged with vibrant life and energy. She loved to be active and did most things with force and vigor. She had little small talk but loved the cut and thrust of serious talk with another able mind. She liked games—especially "The Game" of charades, or Twenty Questions, or Double Crostics—the kinds of games which challenge ingenuity or the mind. She played bridge aggressively, though with too much dash and impulse to make a really good player, and in all of this she loved the contest and she played to win. Edith Pope, one of her best friends in St. Augustine, told the story of her leaning over the bridge table one evening toward her partner, who was playing too languidly for her taste, and uttering two explosive words, which nicely express her whole attitude: "Fight!—Fight!"

She belonged to a generation which was brought up to an unquestioning faith in the doctrine of Success and, though there were many other sides to her nature, one side was always responsive to this ideal. She would not have thought Fitzgerald's remark to Edmund Wilson unusual: "I want to be one of the greatest writers in the world, don't you?" As an exact contemporary of Fitzgerald, she might have made the remark herself. In her younger years she had some of his same innocence, the same bland and bright-eyed expectancy that there was a pot of gold at the end of the rainbow and that she was just the person to find it. Such hopes were based on far more than youthful vanity; from an early age she apparently had an ambience of greatness. Her mother, who in most ways was not soft toward her, had great respect for her poetic gift and let her off from dusting or doing the dishes when she got that "inspired" look in her eye. The 1914 year book of Western High School in Washington described Marjorie Kinnan as "quite the genius of us all," and the class prophecy predicted that she would be the first woman president of the United States. She made the same vivid impression on her contemporaries at the University of Wisconsin who recognized at once from the ease with which she got top grades that she was a "brain," and were quickly made aware of her other talents from the wide swath she cut in dramatic and literary activities. She so easily achieved prominence on campus that after leaving college she was at first puzzled and then increasingly dismayed when the success and acclaim she had so confidently expected failed to materialize. That she eventually found the pot of gold was due as much to sheer luck in moving to Florida and to her doggedness and grit as to her very substantial talents.

In physical appearance she was short, with small hands and feet, but she gave a sense of strength rather than delicacy, of force rather than fragility. She had large, gray-blue eyes with dark, arched brows, and brown hair which had been blondish when she was in college. Her face was round—an enemy would have called her moon-faced—but she had a firm chin, a direct gaze, a small but definite nose, and a way of holding her mouth in a straight, firm line, apparent even in her baby pictures, which gave strength and determination to her whole expression. She had an alert, vital expression, especially when her interest was aroused and her eyes were lighted up, though she cultivated in late years a habit disconcerting to persons who did not know her of turning off the light in her eyes when she was bored and making her face an expressionless mask. People were often surprised on hearing her voice for the first time, expecting because she wrote of the deep South to hear the soft tones of Southern speech, but even though she was raised in Washington, D. C., the stamp of her Wisconsin and New York State years was unmistakable. The voice was Northern and Western—flat, square-cornered, a little hard and nasal.

Her associates on the Wisconsin *Lit* remembered her as slender and a bit prim—Charles Rawlings' nickname for her in their courting days was "Skinny." Ernest L. Meyer said that she wore gloves and high-heeled shoes to their picnics and was careful where she sat down. He was astonished at her first Florida stories because their earthiness did not jibe with his memory of

Marjorie seated on a stump at Picnic Point on Lake Mendota picking an ant from her knee with shuddering abhorrence. The maiden slimness changed with time so that in her middle and later years she was full-bodied and had to fight a running skirmish with diets to control her weight. Herschel Brickell, visiting the Creek one winter, wisecracked to Marjorie that when she was all bundled up ready for the hunt it was hard to tell her from the bear. The fastidiousness gave way to a relative indifference to clothes, and though she liked to dress up she always hated to fuss over what she considered nonessentials. She dressed in much the same fashion as she handled cut flowers, which she would bring into the house in great armfuls, thrust into water without careful arrangement, and let them speak for themselves. The furnishings at Cross Creek reflected the same taste—color, warmth, utility rather than fashionable elegance.

She had a histrionic streak harking back at least to her campus days when she had taken dramatics so seriously that for a time she questioned whether the fame she sought might not be found more readily in the theater than in writing. She decisively gave up the idea of the stage in the early twenties but not a certain dramatic flair which cropped up in many ways during her whole lifetime. She always complained about the tyrannous demands and small rewards of public lecturing, but often accepted speaking engagements; because once over the first nervousness she spoke with great effectiveness, usually disregarding her prepared script in favor of an extemporaneous and informal delivery, and charming her audiences with her warmth and wit. She was also fond of reading aloud at parties from her favorite poets, complete with gestures and posturing. Her fondness for gesture sometimes had a glint of the outlandish about it. She once by mistake dropped one of Charles Rawlings' favorite fishing reels into salt water so that it corroded and was ruined. She made amends by buying a duplicate reel, wrapping it carefully in a waterproof covering, and presenting it to him at dinner on his plate mounded over with mashed potatoes.

The move from Rochester to Cross Creek had something of the grand gesture in it, and to all her other motives must be added her romantic desire to play a role which combined features of several rural myths: that of the sturdy frontierswoman facing the perils of the wilderness, that of the simple farm wife tending her house and garden and barnyard, and that of the female squire riding to the hounds or galloping about on a blooded horse supervising her acres and in the evening acting the gracious hostess in a long gown. Each of these myths got written into her stories and each in some measure she played out in real life. She learned how little country life resembles the myths about it, and she often spoke about the grievous contrast between the *idea* in Rochester of running an orange grove and the *fact* of running the grove, where insects, drought, windstorm, and freeze all compromised the pleasant pastoral vision she had before she came. She learned from experience the old truism that it is possible to believe in pastoral idylls in direct proportion to one's distance from the dung heap. One surviving photograph shows her dressed in a draggled cotton frock and white lisle stockings, her hair stringy, squatting on a low stool with her forehead pressed against a cow's flank while she does the milking, and something about the picture implies a temper frayed by weariness, flies, and heat. She was a large enough spirit so that knowing its harshness she could still love the rural life and still hold fast to some of her original vision of its idyllic beauty and grace.

Because she wrote convincingly of hunting, fishing, and the out-of-doors, she produced in the public mind an image of herself as a kind of great white huntress. Legend still current around Cross Creek has it that she was a fabulous shot with a gun, though most such stories are traceable to a single unreliable source, the old Negro Will Mickens, who lived in the tenant house at the grove. "I'm afraid of that woman with a gun," he'd say. "She could cut a thread with a .22 or shoot the head off a moccasin at sixty feet." The fact is that Marjorie was a poor shot and freely admitted it, and her participation in vigorous outdoor sports was quite limited. She had no record of achievement or even of much participation in sports of any kind before coming to Cross Creek. She had tramped in the woods with her father, but she was not particularly talented in physical skills, was only a mediocre swimmer and horsewoman, and had scarcely hunted so much as a rabbit. This makes all the more remarkable her activities at Cross Creek. When she moved to Florida she put on willingness like a coat, and for about ten years, from 1928 to 1938, she tried every vigorous activity the new life had to offer. "All this strenuous out-door stuff," she wrote to Perkins, "is new to me since coming to Florida. I've taken to it naturally, but my chief claim to capability in such matters lies only in being game for anything" [MKR to MEP March 3, 1933]. She entered into the deer hunts, the crab-fishing, and frog-gigging as she entered into the fish fries, the square dances, and other cracker "doings" —in an exploratory spirit, eager to discover and record the essence of this new way of life.

As she began to write about Florida, the hunting and related activities became "research" in the broad sense, like the weeks she spent in the scrub helping to run a moonshine still. She always maintained the detachment of an interested observer but had no cynicism; she knew she was playing a kind of glorious game, but she did so with utter sincerity, and her deepest motives went beyond a search for adventure to a search for the truth of the people and the way of life she had decided to make into literature. Partly through lack of experience, partly because of her dramatic sense, she was always mildly self-conscious in boots and breeches, which she wore as if they were a costume, and she held her gun in the crook of her arm and went through the other motions of hunting as if they were gestures in a ritual to which she was not fully habituated. The killing involved in the hunt became less and less bearable to her as time passed and at last she put up her guns altogether, but she never gave up tramping in the woods, nor her passionate love for every natural process. She loved hunting because it got her up before dawn when she could snuff the early morning smells, hear the first twitter and rustle of waking birds, and watch the growing light. She loved the hearty man-talk, the belling of the dogs, the cold air, the wood smoke and whiskey and tobacco, the whole pageantry and gusto of the experience. She tried all kinds, from duck hunting in freezing blinds on Orange Lake to bear hunting in the scrub, but always as one who tastes and savors the quality of experience rather than as a true *aficionado.*

Her originality and independence are sufficiently clear from her dramatic forsaking of the city and a whole way of life to move to Cross Creek; her considerable physical courage is plain from her decision to stay on alone in so remote a place and run the grove after her divorce. Though she was an unusually sensitive and imaginative person, she was afraid of nothing—except for snakes, a fear which she partly got over after a snake hunt with Ross Allen in the Everglades. She had a marked earthiness in her nature and like many artists a Keatsian joy in the senses, a love of good food and drink, of company and conviviality, and she had great gifts as a hostess. She wished everyone who visited the Creek to share her own enthusiasm for the beauties and pleasures of life there, and she took her guests deer hunting or duck hunting in season, went deep-sea fishing with them on the Gulf or the Atlantic, set up river trips on the Oklawaha and Withlacoochee, took them into the scrub on nature hikes or out on Orange Lake to catch largemouth bass. A glance at *Cross Creek Cookery* or at the chapter in *Cross Creek* entitled "Our Daily Bread" will show that in the kitchen and in the dining room she was "Epicurus' own daughter." She fed her guests both exquisitely and prodigiously from her own kitchen with a skill approaching a fine art, and in this area too she was willing to try anything, from broiled alligator tail to the most sophisticated pastries and soufflés. She poured out with a free hand her prime corn whiskey made by her friends in the scrub and mellowed in a charred oak cask in the attic above her bedroom closet. It was a formidable and unforgettable experience to be a guest at Cross Creek and Marjorie loved every minute of pleasure she gave, even though her conscience often twinged because of the writing she neglected to see to her guests.

She sometimes could indulge a mood of sheer exuberance, as when Charles Rawlings sold his first Tarpon Springs story to "the Boston Bastards," as they endearingly called the *Atlantic Monthly*. They uncorked a jug of 'shine, turned loose all the game chickens and guinea fowl, and had a hunt with .22 rifles as long as there was a bird in sight—which was more sporting than it sounds considering Marjorie's poor marksmanship. Her sense of humor was one of her most attractive qualities; she had a quick smile and no reluctance to indulge in a belly laugh. She could turn a quip as well as a racy story or on occasion indulge an elfin taste for practical jokes. One evening at a dignified party in St. Augustine she slipped a silk stocking into the coat pocket of James Branch Cabell so that a generous length of it dangled in plain sight. He discovered it only after he had unwittingly displayed it to nearly everyone at the party while Marjorie silently dissolved with laughter in the background. He was terribly miffed, as was his wife, and Marjorie had to be abject in a letter of apology the next day.

In typically American fashion, her earthiness was combined with its opposite, a haunting puritanism, so that within her as twin brother to the pagan bacchante dwelt an ascetic with a stern sense of duty and a strict morality, to whom the great abstractions of piety and justice, honor and purity and temperance, were compelling laws. She could use profanity with relish and good effect, and she loved to swap off-color stories, which she could tell with great skill, but deep inside she retained a paradoxically chaste and virginal reserve. She spoke with great frankness about sex, but wrote about sex chiefly as a biological, creative process relating to animal life and not as sensuous experience relating to human life. Her attempts in her stories to portray mature sexual love between adults are few and notably unsuccessful.

In cast of mind she resembled the great transcendentalists of the last century; she had the same moral earnestness, the same essential idealism and optimism, the same intuitive depth. Her mind was quick and alert and well-stocked from a good education and extensive reading, but while she had a meditative turn, she was not philosophical in the sense that she thought habitually in a systematic, orderly fashion. Her mind, like Emerson's, was essentially poetic rather than systematic. It tended to convert intellectual concepts into concrete images or metaphors, worked in bright electric flashes, and was closely geared to her intuitive powers and to her emotions. She learned quickly and had a roving perpetual inquisitiveness so that she continued to grow intellectually during her whole lifetime. Perkins said that he never saw anyone learn so much from a first novel—and he might have added, from a second novel, for *Golden Apples* in some ways taught her more than *South Moon Under.* She read with great rapidity and retentiveness, and on occasion went on reading orgies in which she would pull the blinds and work her way through a whole stack of books, ignoring night or day, and pausing only to sleep and eat.

Far more than intellect, the true center of her nature was a cluster of nonrational faculties of which intuition, emotion, and will were the most important. She had too many anchors to earth to be a mystic, but she had a deep and active intuitive sense which she constantly heeded, and she had at least one authentic mystic experience. While she was sitting alone in the University of Wisconsin library one afternoon, she felt bathed in a sense of vibration, a pulsation of light or waves of force which gave her an ecstatic feeling of great warmth and joy. This was not an hallucination, she retained complete, even heightened consciousness, except that when it was over she could not recall how long the sensation had lasted. This became one of the central experiences of her life and she referred to it as her "glimpse of eternity." On the day late in the fall of 1930 when she was lost for several hours in the scrub and felt the unmitigated silence of the wilderness press in upon her, and had the experience so rare to modern man of nakedly confronting the primordial heart of nature with no mediating buffer of civilization—no roads, no vehicles, no lights or sounds, no signaling systems, not even the presence of another human being—on that day also she felt no fear but a suffusion of joy and healing calm something like a mystic elation.

For all her love of people and conviviality she had also a hunger for solitude which went unfed in cities, and this was one of the great reasons why she made the move to Cross Creek and why she chose to stay there alone after her separation from

Charles Rawlings. It was also one of the reasons she had great difficulty adjusting to life in St. Augustine after her marriage to Norton Baskin. In 1933 she said to an interviewer from the New York *Herald-Tribune:* "I think . . . I am what is called a hermit. If I had to choose between trees and people I think I should choose trees" [Elizabeth Shepley Sergeant, "A Visit to a Hermit in the Big Scrub. . . ." New York *Herald Tribune Books*, June 18, 1933]. With its acrid note of misanthropy, this sounds like Thoreau, but it is too extreme to be characteristic of Marjorie and was no doubt prompted by the hurt she was feeling from the separation from her first husband, but she undoubtedly always was something of a hermit. On those infrequent occasions when she went to New York to consult her publisher or to have a medical check-up at the Harkness Pavilion, she could remain in the city only for a few days before she began to feel a terrible restlessness and an almost compulsive desire to get away again to the country. Closeness to nature was as essential to her as to the great romantics and like them she had a feeling for the life in plants or rocks, in hills or in a river, which resembled the animism of primitive folk. With Thoreau she could easily have believed that a pine tree when cut down might go to a higher heaven than herself.

She shared the religious uncertainty of many modern writers, having deep religious sensibilities but no formal commitment. As a child she had gone with her family to a Baptist church in Washington; and later at the University of Wisconsin, already breaking a tenuous church connection, she seldom attended services, though she sometimes went to a Congregational church near campus "to do my praying." After college she made the break with the church definite and final and once wrote to Charles Rawlings that she found religious matters "morbid" and full of outworn superstition. She had something like a religious attachment to a concept which she called the "cosmic consciousness," resembling Whitman's pantheism or the transcendentalist doctrine of the oversoul. This was her intuitive, half-ecstatic awareness that birth, growth, and death are one and good, and that the life which moved the stars was the same life which breathed through the forest and beat in her own heart. She felt that the best way to know this life was to live as close as possible to nature, or at least to some plot of earth where one could sense its great simple rhythms. Her years at Cross Creek, when she came closest to living in this fashion, were her own most fruitful and in some ways her happiest years.

For all the forcefulness and strength of her character, she had a very feminine tendency to answer the promptings of her emotions, and these were warm and tender to the point of sentimentality. She often regretted being childless, though not in the fashion of some women where the whole life is darkened by a sense of irretrievable loss. She was particularly fond of little boys, more so than of girls, and on two occasions came within a breath of adopting a son, but was deterred in one case by entanglements with the boy's family, in the other by religious considerations raised by officious bureaucrats.

Like other artists she was egoistic, and on occasion she could be—"bitchy" would be her own word—but there was little meanness in her nature. Philip May, her lawyer who knew her as a friend for years before working closely with her during the Cross Creek Trial, called her "great-hearted," and generosity in the largest sense was one of her most obvious traits. She loved to do for people and took an almost childish delight in sending gifts and surprises. One of the universal remembrances of her around Cross Creek is of her open heart and open hand. Toward people of all kinds she was *simpatico*, she loved them, was genuinely interested in them, and felt a true sympathy and compassion for them. People sensed this in her and usually responded in kind. For a person of her northern, college-bred, city background to be accepted as one of themselves by the people of Cross Creek is a major personal triumph, but it was not only among simple country people that she found such acceptance. Her correspondence reflects an acquaintance of the most astonishing variety. Some letters to her are a semi-literate, penciled scrawl on ruled paper; some have the splashy letterhead of a major movie studio, some are on the crisply elegant stationery of the White House, or of a famous artist, or of an

English lord. All address her with the same voice of respect, admiration, and affection.

Because her emotions were strong and near the surface, she often acted more on impulse than on reasoned judgment, and her idealism often led her to adopt strong but ingenuous positions toward complex issues. She was invited to address the Woman's Club of Gainesville one evening in the late thirties and chose to speak in the most uncompromising fashion about the necessity of granting Negroes complete social and political equality. Her good friend Dr. John Tigert, president of the University of Florida, told her tartly afterward that she had more courage than sense. Her own stance toward the Negro had gone through several stages before she arrived at the opinion she expressed that night. When she first moved to Florida, the rural Negroes were so alien that she was at a loss as to how to take them, and her early notes are full of the callous-seeming phrases of a stock response: "grinning black ape," "monkey-like paw." When she began to know these Negroes as individual human beings in all their variety, she made her own firm decision that they should be treated simply like other human beings. "Just turn them all loose!" she once exclaimed to Julia Scribner Bigham. In her own writing she did exactly that, representing them as she saw them, some as scoundrels and plain trash, others as gentle and noble and humane. Zora Neale Hurston, a Negress who herself wrote fine novels about Florida, and one of Marjorie's devoted friends, complimented her once on the unusual honesty of her depiction of Negroes. It is typical that, having made a decision on a controversial issue like racial prejudice, Marjorie should be unflinching, even unpolitic in asserting her view. She could involve herself with eager delight in all the little personal intrigues which penetrated human relations in a small community like Cross Creek, but on issues she was almost incapable of duplicity or even of compromise.

She herself knew about the importance of emotion in her nature. While she was at work on *Cross Creek* she wrote to Ellen Glasgow, "I have been working very hard on my book, so hard that I put myself in the hospital for a week. It wouldn't seem necessary to tie oneself into knots to get out a few ideas, but while I *feel* at the drop of a hat, thinking is terribly hard work for me" [MKR to EG July 19, 1941]. She wrote to Perkins once that all she really had to offer in her books was "a certain emotional sincerity"—a remark which was entirely too self-effacing, for her books contain far more substance than this implies and in other moods she knew it. It is true that her judgments as a literary critic were sometimes untrustworthy, because even though she was capable of the most penetrating insights she often allowed emotional bias to affect her judgment, particularly if a work was by someone she liked. Her generosity toward people had a rare coverage in extending to other writers; she had almost no professional jealousy, but genuinely rejoiced in the achievements of others, and she had a habit of dashing off warm letters of praise to authors whose books she had enjoyed.

Beneath all her genial qualities, beneath the humor, the idealism, the generosity, and love of life, lay a stratum of melancholy which is apparent as early as the 1920's and which grew larger as she grew older. Because she had a strong prejudice against pictures of grinning female authors, almost all of the surviving photographs of her show her in unsmiling poses, but in her later pictures there is a haunting pervasive melancholy to the expression. Shortly before her death Carl Van Vechten took a series of photographs of her and, since their brief friendship had consisted chiefly of pleasant exchanges of light banter, he was surprised when he developed the pictures. "I didn't know about the tragedy," he said, "until I saw the photographs. It's a tragic face." This dark strand in her life was similar to what is now fashionably called existential despair and apparently had no specific content except that she suffered most from it when the writing was going badly. In a letter to her friend Norman Berg in 1946, she said, "What happens is that a great deal of the time I am in contact with the cosmic warmth or the cosmic vitality. As long as the strong current flows through me, I can work, I am *aware*. Then suddenly the lights go out. I am lost and in despair" [MKR to NB May 4, 1946]. This is the same dark mood she had detected in Fitzgerald ten years earlier, something she had slipped deeply enough into herself by the early thirties that she had begun to try alcohol to take off the edge of the pain it caused, and as the pain persisted and increased so did the drinking, until by the forties she was a definite alcoholic. The puritan in her was deeply offended by what it saw as grave weakness in such behavior, and she fought against the drinking but never with more than temporary success. One is reminded of the large number of her contemporaries—Lardner, Fitzgerald, Faulkner, Hemingway, to cite only a few—whose souls apparently received impulses on this same dark wave-length of despair and who also used alcohol to moderate the pain they felt.

Carl Gustav Jung developed in one of his later books the theory that every creative person is a duality, on the one side a human being with the common longing for happiness, satisfaction, and security, and on the other side a creative process—a ruthless impersonal passion for creativity which is in conflict with the human being and seeks to dominate him and make him its instrument. To the extent which the creative force predominates, the human being is molded by it and rendered a helpless observer of events it cannot control, and for this reason the lives of poets are usually full of pain and tragedy. "There are hardly any exceptions to the rule," said Jung, "that a person must pay dearly for the divine gift of creative fire [*Modern Man in Search of a Soul*, chapter VIII]. It would be too simple to explain the tragedy in Marjorie Kinnan Rawlings' life, particularly the unhappiness of her later years, solely in terms of this theory. For one thing Jung was thinking of the great towering genius like Goethe when he developed his theory, and she was no such genius. She did have a substantial talent, and beyond question was driven by that talent to write, so that there was a cleavage in her life of the sort Jung describes, and in understanding her one must be concerned with both the woman and the artist. Her pain was not that of the artist possessed by a *furor poeticus* so great it consumes the vessel which contains it. Hers was much more the pathos of the artist whose divine fire would not burn brightly enough. John Steinbeck once asked her if she didn't find it harder to write as she grew older, and she admitted that it was, and was relieved to discover that someone else beside herself found it so. But for the last ten years of her life she tried by sheer force of will to blow that fire to a brighter flame, and for fuel she used the tender substance of that other human side of her nature, so that it is not difficult to collect anecdotes of drunken or unseemly behavior from her last years. Like a true artist she wrote because she had to, and all her life the words came hard, but she would not give up because they came hard. From the struggle the artist in her produced a number of truly luminous works of art, and when one stands in a place where he can see all her single traits forming one pattern, the woman who contained the artist always evokes the same phrase. She was "great-hearted."

4

The Florida Eden

As a "Southern" regionalist Marjorie Kinnan Rawlings was unique in having the insider's commitment of love for place, but also the outsider's objectivity, so that she could write of her chosen home with passion and sympathy but without the film of bias or prejudice peculiar to the place. Like Faulkner she could feel drawn to the past, but she was not haunted by a specifically Southern past with its Lost Cause and "peculiar institution." She could be an agrarian but without that nostalgia for the antebellum way of life which shaded the writings of Ransom, Tate, and the other members of the Nashville group. In Faulkner's *Absalom, Absalom!* Quentin Compson is asked by his Canadian friend Shreve what it was like to live in the South. "You can't understand," was his reply. "You would have to be born there." Such an inside view makes possible kinds of knowing forever closed to an outsider, but the opposite is also true. Some kinds of knowing are possible for the outsider which are forever closed to the one born within. The newcomer, because he can never entirely relinquish his past, will always view his chosen home, no matter how familiar it may become or how deep his love for it, with a kind of binocular vision which sharpens the outlines and deepens the dimensions of what he sees. He cannot help his vision being a continuous evaluation, a running comparison or contrast where objects of his adopted world can never be taken for granted, but must always be seen under the aspect of the old. It was in this fashion that Marjorie looked upon her part of Florida.

She was probably no more dependent upon personal experience for the raw materials of her art than most other twentieth-century writers of fiction, no more certainly than Joyce, Hemingway, Faulkner, or Fitzgerald; but after she had achieved a measure of popular success she was haunted by the fear that she might be remembered by posterity as a *mere* regionalist, as no more than the chronicler of the Florida backwoods. That many of the most distinguished poets and writers of her time were also regionalists did not remove the burden of her discontent. Robert Frost had no objection to being called a New England poet, because he knew that the "New Englandness" of his poems was only the beginning and not the end of their possible meanings. William Faulkner discovered early in his career that he would never live long enough to exhaust the literary possibilities of his "little postage stamp of earth," and under the incredible fertility of his imagination the created domain of Yoknapatawpha County became a territory amply spacious for one of the largest literary designs of the present century. But when Marjorie discovered the little-known backwoods area of north central Florida, then fell in love with it, and for twelve years made literature from the excitement of this love affair, she was at last unwilling to settle for her little postage stamp of earth. She had a theory that the truly great writer should be able to take material from any time or place and convert it into art, and to prove she was that kind of artist she spent more than ten painful years on *The Sojourner* with its northern setting. She might have spared herself the pain. Fame has many faces, but fame for Marjorie Kinnan Rawlings wears the lean tanned features of a Florida cracker, and no other. Whatever lasting reputation she achieves will grow inevitably from *The Yearling, Cross Creek, South Moon Under,* and the other Florida stories, and it is primarily as a regionalist that she will be remembered.

Even when the attempt is made to confine it to literature, "regionalism" is a slippery term, because it has been variously conceived and because it combines so readily with other elements, political, social, or economic. For the present purpose, regionalism is best seen as one extension of modern literary realism, whose hallmark is an attachment to a particular geographic area. One of its main intentions is to set forth the physical characteristics of that area, its legends and historic past, its people with their way of life, their speech, their peculiarities of culture. There is no reason why "regional" should not apply to city novels and stories, but usually the term has suggested the rural, the agrarian, or the pastoral, just as the opposite nationalist or collectivist tendency in literature has been identified with the city and has implied an attitude of urbane haughtiness toward "the sticks."

The continuous American search for a national identity has produced in literature, as in politics, alternating cycles of emphasis on the local and the national, and the history of American literature shows several peaks in regionalist writing, one occurring shortly after the Civil War, and another, more fruitful in the production of significant literary works, after World War I, during the late twenties and thirties. The early part of the present century saw an aggressive attack on the rural, with many writers bitterly criticizing the narrowness and the cultural barrenness of village life, an attack which became particularly shrill with such writers as Mencken and Sinclair Lewis. But the Wall Street crash of 1929 and the Great Depression reversed the great surge of business expansion and the confident materialism and dominant urban attitudes which were part of it. Economic catastrophe and social unrest produced a widespread renewal of interest in the regions, so that life in the village began to receive new scrutiny as a source of those virtues which could heal the ills brought on by too much city and too much big business.

Marjorie's flight from Rochester in 1928 corresponds almost exactly in its timing with the larger wave of reaction from megalopolis. Her books, as regionalist writings, were part of a major literary movement which included literally hundreds of other titles. Howard W. Odum and Henry E. Moore estimate in their broad study of American regionalism that between 1927 and 1938 some 1,500 regionalist novels were published in America, a count which excludes a much larger number of short fictions. Of the twenty-two Pulitzer Prizes for fiction awarded in the years between the two World Wars, fifteen were for regionalist works; and to name the writers who published at least one regionalist title during the twelve years of Marjorie's most active writing career (1931-1942) is to call the roll of the most distinguished writers of the time—Faulkner, Wolfe, Steinbeck, Ellen Glasgow, John P. Marquand, Erskine Caldwell, R. P. Warren, Sherwood Anderson, to mention only a few.

Possibly because she was tender on this subject, she accepted several invitations to speak on topics related to regionalism. Most notably she wrote a paper entitled, "Regional Literature of the South," for the 1939 annual convention of the National Council of Teachers of English in New York City. She opened her remarks with a salty condemnation of the phrase "regional literature," which she called an illegitimate, recent coinage referring to "futile outpourings of bad writing whose only excuse is that they are regional, regionalism being at the moment a popular form of expression." She argued that the only legitimate regionalist writings were serious scientific or sociological studies such as might be written for the *National Geographic* or for doctoral dissertations. Fiction which merely exploits quaint customs or local color is spurious, a betrayal of the people it represents, and undeserving of the name of literature. "The producer of literature," she said, "is not a reporter but a creator. His concern is not with presenting the superficial and external aspects, however engaging, of an actual people. It is with the inner revelation of mankind, thinking and moving against the backdrop of life itself. . . ." The artist's contribution of imagination is needed to transform regional materials into art, and it is the artist's talent, not the materials, which determined the degree of artistry. "If [the artist] writes well he is almost independent of material, for his genius is able to transmute dross into gold. . . . Yet the best writing is implicit with a profound harmony between the writer and his material so that many of the greatest books of all time are regionalist books, in which the artist used for his own artistic purposes, a background that he loved and deeply understood. Thomas Hardy is a compelling instance."

Thus she knew perfectly well that the term "regionalist," if it could be applied to so great a writer as Hardy, need carry no stigma; yet still she was sensitive, possibly because she was aware that she had worked on both sides of the fence which divides local color from literature. She knew that her first Florida writing, "Cracker Chidlings," was little more than inspired reportage, and she remembered the letters from Perkins urging her to revise *South Moon Under* so as to diminish the social chronicle and give more emphasis to story and character. She also knew that, though she had stumbled with *Golden Apples*, the strongest parts of that book had been the regionalist parts, and she now had the deepest confidence that in *The Yearling* she had been able to transmute regionalist materials into a new substance which was unmistakably art.

Her literary world was comprised chiefly of the rural portion of three counties in north central Florida—Alachua, Putnam, and Marion—and culturally within this area was restricted mainly to the life of the poor-white natives, the so-called crackers. This country, its landforms and its waters, its plants and animals, its seasons and weather, and above all its people and their whole way of life she rendered with unusual depth and accuracy. The area is part of that region where the northern temperate zone passes into the semitropics so that it contains trees, shrubs, and flowers of both zones. Though it gives the general impression of flatness, it contains many low rolling hills and small creek and river valleys and is heavily wooded with pine and cypress and various hardwoods over much of its surface. Farming was carried on during the years of Marjorie's residence chiefly on small diversified farms whose main crops were those of the lower South—corn, tobacco, peanuts, truck crops, and some cotton. In the early thirties she was witness to a major transition in the Florida cattle industry, the closing of the open range by statewide fence laws and the gradual replacement of the wild longhorned scrub cattle with blooded stock fattened on improved pastures and feed lots. In this experience of the closing of the range, she had a brush with the legendary wild West, which she wrote into several of her stories, quite aware all the while that she was seeing the passing of one era and the opening of another.

The raising of citrus is given so prominent a place in her writings that one might imagine her living in the very heart of citrus country. Actually, her land at Cross Creek lay on the northern fringe of the citrus belt and her groves were very nearly the northernmost commercial groves in the state. Partially buffered from cold by two large lakes, they were survivors of the disastrous freezes of 1894-95, which drove the major portion of the industry further south to frostfree areas along the central ridge of the state. Her groves were small by present-day standards—only forty-odd acres—but they produced a thin-skinned, high quality fruit, and were at one time a highly profitable enterprise when the market was based upon quality fresh-fruit shipments rather than quantity production for concentrate plants. Although Orange Lake and Lake Lochloosa afforded some protection from winter cold, Marjorie saw her whole crop wiped out by freezes at least four times during her years at Cross Creek and severely damaged on other occasions. Part of her unusual sensitivity to weather and the flow of the seasons was undoubtedly the farmer's ability to feel in his own body the effect of wind and rain and sun upon the crops he has committed to the elements. When she first moved to Florida she thought of her property not primarily as a citrus grove, but as a farm in the Yankee sense, a diversified farm on which citrus would be the main cash crop as apples might be the main crop in New

York State. She meant to raise truck crops and chickens and pecans as well as citrus, and actually did undertake commercial plantings of green pepper, string beans, and eggplant during the early thirties. It was only after several years of residence that she began to refer habitually to her place in the customary Florida fashion as "the grove."

In terms of their Florida setting, her stories fall into two groups—those based on the Cross Creek area, and those based upon the Big Scrub. The Cross Creek locale is most fully realized in the book bearing that name, but many features of this countryside are discernible in the early novelette, "Jacob's Ladder," in *Golden Apples,* and in a number of the short stories. "Jacob's Ladder" is a virtual travelogue of north central Florida, following the movements of a young cracker couple, Mart and Florrie, from the flat piney woods of Dixie County above the Suwannee River, to Orange Lake in Alachua County, to the mouth of a tidal river on the Gulf of Mexico (probably the Withlacoochee), to the Big Scrub, and finally back to Dixie County. The central scene in *Golden Apples,* the hammock land where Luke and Allie find refuge as squatters and to which the Englishman Tordell is exiled by his family, is closely patterned upon her own grove at Cross Creek. The other main features of topography in the book are likewise reproduced faithfully from real life—the fictional town of Purley is the real town of Island Grove; the great orange groves of Camilla Van Dyne on the western shore of Orange Lake were suggested by the Samson Groves in MacIntosh, Florida; Orange Lake appears as Sawgrass Lake, while Lake Lochloosa and the River Styx appear prominently in the story under their own names. Cross Creek landscape is discernible also in many of the short stories, particularly in the Quincy Dover stories where Marjorie began to evolve a fictional world based on the town of Oak Bluff, which seems to be a composite of the three towns nearest to her—Hawthorne, Island Grove, and Citra.

The other main locus of her fiction is the Ocala Scrub, or Big Scrub, a semi-wilderness area located about twenty-five miles south and east of Cross Creek between the Oklawaha and St. Johns rivers. Some fifty miles long and twenty-five miles wide, the scrub is nearly identical with the present Ocala National Forest. Marjorie describes the area with vivid accuracy in the opening pages of *South Moon Under:*

The Florida scrub was unique. . . . There was perhaps no similar region anywhere. It was a vast dry rectangular plateau, bounded on three sides by two rivers. The Oklawaha, flowing towards the north, bounded it on the west. At the north-west corner of the rectangle the Oklawaha turned sharply at right angles and flowed due east, joining, at the north-east corner, the St. Johns River which formed the eastern demarcation.

Within these deep watery lines the scrub stood aloof, uninhabited through its wider reaches. The growth repelled all human living. The soil was a tawny sand, from whose parched infertility there reared, indifferent to water, so dense a growth of scrub pine—the Southern spruce—that the effect of the massed thin trunks was of a limitless, canopied stockade. It seemed impenetrable, for a man-high growth of scrub oak, myrtle, sparkleberry and ti-ti filled the interstices. Wide areas, indeed, admitted of no human passage.

In places the pines grew more openly, the sunlight filtered through and patches of ground showed bald and lichened. The scrub was sparingly dotted with small lakes and springs. Around these grew a damp-loving hammock vegetation. Or a random patch of moisture produced, alien in the dryness, a fine stand of slash pine or long-leaf yellow. These were known as pine islands. To any one standing on a rise, they were visible from a great distance.

The scrub rolled towards its boundaries like a dark sea. It cast itself against the narrow beach of swamp and hammock that fringed the rivers. The two types of growth did not mingle, as though an ascetic race withdrew itself from a tropical one and refused to inter-breed. The moisture along the rivers gave a footing for the lush growth of cypress in the swamp; of live oak, magnolia, hickory, ash, bay, sweet gum and holly that made up the adjoining hammock.

The western edge of the scrub plateau was high. The Oklawaha ran forty or fifty feet below, so that its scrub-side bank rose from the river swamp in a steep ledge [*SMU*, 2-3].

This unusual landscape Marjorie utilized for the setting of her first novel, *South Moon Under*, and for her most famous novel, *The Yearling*, and for a number of short stories. She continually emphasizes the silence of the scrub, its wildness and loneliness, its lack of inhabitants, and its generally forbidding aspect to those unfamiliar with it. The primordial wildness of the scrub had a strong appeal for her; she liked the notion that there never had been human habitation in the true scrub and probably never would be, that she might cross where no man had ever crossed before. Because the soil was dry and sandy, there had been little to attract pioneer farmers into the area during the nineteenth century when other parts of central Florida were being settled; and after the big cypress had been cut from along the Oklawaha River, there was little to attract capitalists, so that when Marjorie first knew the scrub in the early 1930's, hardly more than half a dozen families lived in it except for small settlements along the Oklawaha and at Lake Kerr. It had remained literally a frontier area where a man could still make a living with an axe and a gun.

In her passion for authenticity she acquired extensive knowledge of the history of the scrub and used accurately a number of historical references in her stories. The devastating northeaster which blew for nearly a week in 1871 and flooded many parts of the scrub became a central event in *The Yearling*. The Riverside settlement established on the banks of the Oklawaha, but abandoned after the 1895 freeze, was referred to in several stories. In depicting the landscape itself, she adjusted her description carefully to note seasonal variation in the growth of trees and flowers. She had the same sensitivity as Thoreau to the flow of the seasons and, as he had done in *Walden*, used a cycle of the seasons as one of the main organizing devices of her own book, *Cross Creek*. She said she could tell the stage of spring by the particular scent of the citrus, "for the seasons at the Creek are marked, not by the calendar, but by fruits and flowers and birds." In similar fashion, her descriptions of the scrub are always phased into a floral calendar. *The Yearling* encompasses one full year, with each season accurately distin-

guished, as in the following passage which details late summer:

In a late afternoon toward the end of August, Jody went with the fawn to the sink-hole for fresh water for supper. The road was bright with flowers. The sumac was in bloom, and the colic root sent up tall stalks of white or orange orchid-like flowers. The French mulberries were beginning to ripen on slim stems. They were lavender in color, close-clustered, like snails' eggs along lily stalks. Butterflies sat on the first purple buds of the fragrant deer-tongue, opening and closing their wings slowly, as though waiting for the buds to open and the nectar to be revealed. The covey call of quail sounded again from the pea-field, clear and sweet and communal [*Y*, 216].

She knew best two portions of the scrub where she herself had lived, and it is these areas that she uses in her books. The first of these, the setting of *South Moon Under*, runs along the Oklawaha River from Moss Bluff north to Orange Springs and centers on the home of Leonard Fiddia and his mother Piety, which was located in the scrub on a bluff above the river about five miles northeast of the crossroads town of Eureka. This area she presents in great detail, naming accurately many points along the river—Tobacco Patch Landing, Big Saw Grass, Hog-Thief Creek—and this remarkably beautiful river itself she treats fully. The Oklawaha is an unusually swift stream for Florida, red-brown, deep and clear, flowing with many sharp bends past high bluffs on the scrub side and through moss-hung cypress swamps until it joins the St. Johns River between Welaka and Lake George. Marjorie had an especial love for the waterways in her part of Florida, the Suwannee, the Waccasassa, the Withlacoochee, as well as the Oklawaha and the St. Johns. They had for her an exotic beauty which was almost literally unearthly, and she records on several occasions her sense that whenever she floated on the surface of one of these rivers she had left the world and was drifting in a place where time was somehow suspended.

In *South Moon Under* the Oklawaha becomes almost as much a unifying presence as the scrub itself. In sharing the life of the Fiddia family, Marjorie had learned a great deal about

larjorie Kinnan Rawlings

HER FRIENDS

(RON SHERMAN PHOTO)

het Crosby, grove manager, hunting companion, and good friend

(RON SHERMAN PHOTO)

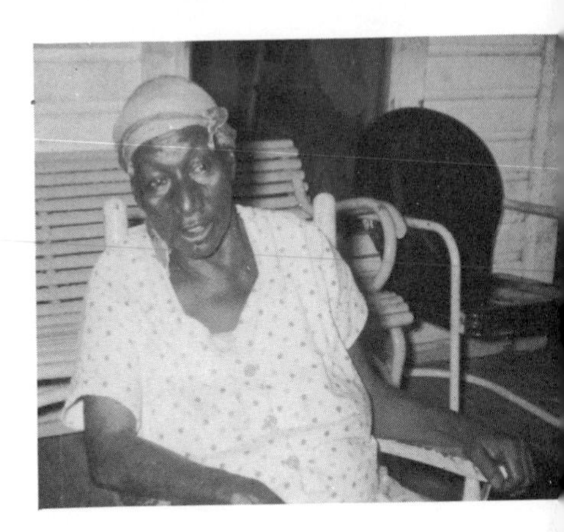

Top: "Uncle" Will Mickens
Above: "Aunt" Martha Mickens (1961)
Left: "Aunt" Martha's daughter Adrenna
Below: Leonard ("Lant") Fiddia and a friend (c. 1935)

Marjorie Kinnan Rawlings
PORTRAIT OF A WOMAN

Above: At the University of Wisconsin, c. 1918
Upper right: At Cross Creek in the middle 1930's
Right: At Salt Springs, c. 1941 (during filming of *The Yearling*)

Above: With her pointer Moe at Crescent Beach in the late 1940's
Right: A publicity photograph taken about 1950

(ERICH HARTMANN PHOTO)

Marjorie Kinnan Rawlings

HER FRONTIER EDEN

Upper left: One of "those preposterous creatures"
Upper right: Cross Creek, looking east toward Lochloosa
Center: The River Styx at north end of Orange Lake
Bottom: Cross Creek

the river, for her cracker friends fished on it, hunted 'gators and trapped along its banks, and they used it as much as the dirt road running through the scrub for a highway. She knew not only the main river, but some of the dark silent tributary creeks as well. She had poled up a number of these streams on 'gator hunts with Leonard, and on one of them, which she calls Taylor's Dread in the book, she had helped to tend a moonshine still. The chapters of this book where Lant, with old Ramrod Simpson, floats cypress log rafts down the river to the mill at Palatka contain some of the finest river sequences since Mark Twain:

They drifted day and night. He took turns with Ramrod at napping in the day-time. The weather turned warm, the current slowed, the river was sun-shot and sleepy. The afternoons were hot. Blue-johns flapped languidly ahead and vultures did not stir from their roosts. The river edge was a bronze mirror.

There came a time in mid-afternoon when all life seemed suspended. The river flowed interminably but as though without advance. The boy thought that he had been always in this still, liquid place. There was no change. There was no memory and no imagining. . . . Nothing existed but the brown, clear water, flowing in one spot forever. Ramrod sat hunched at the oar-bench; lunatic, insensate; silent at the sweep. The water lettuce whirled slowly around and around, like dancers waltzing in their sleep. Lant watched until he drowsed with it; around and around and around. . . .

They had waited for a full moon for the trip and the river was as plain as by day. Lant liked the swirling progress in the moonlight between the dark banks. . . . He could see water-turkies and limpkins roosting high in the cypresses. Wood-ducks lifted from the coves with a wild rush of wings and herons, disturbed at their slumber, flew ahead of the raft, snow-white in the silver brightness. Owls quavered from the shore. He breathed sparingly, listening to the river sucking at the raft, smelling the rank sweetness of the swamps [*SMU*, 164-65].

The second area of the scrub which she treats in detail in her books is *The Yearling* country, centered on a pine island known in real life as Pat's Island—the Baxter's Island of the book—

located about two miles west of Silver Glen Springs which rises near the shore of Lake George. Marjorie lived at Pat's Island on two occasions for a total of nearly four weeks with the family of Cal Long, and in this way she came to know the eastern sector of the scrub intimately. The Baxter place in the novel was modeled closely on the Long homestead—a cypress-shingled frame house and barn and smokehouse with about thirty acres of cleared ground surrounded by split rail fence and located close to a great limestone sink where seepage provided the chief source of water. Many other features of this section of the scrub are detailed in the book—Juniper Springs a few miles to the south with its creek which runs through dense forest before breaking out into a marshy, green valley and emptying into Lake George; Salt Springs, ten miles to the northeast; the frontier trading posts of Ft. Gates and Volusia on the St. Johns.

Marjorie's habit of viewing people against a background makes the settings in her books particularly important, and the air of truth in her best stories is grounded on her intimate, personal acquaintance with the countryside about which she wrote and her passionate interest in the world of nature. She was something like Bartram in reporting for her generation the natural wonders of her part of Florida—the floating islands of Orange Lake, the great crystalline springs, the silent, moss-hung rivers, the profusion of birds and flowers, the strange reptiles. As long as she lived in this country she felt some of that pleasurable throb of mystery which the tropics have always aroused in persons born in colder climates, and she wrote into her books her own continuous sense of wonder at the rich natural beauty with which she was surrounded. But her books were more than enthusiastic travelogues, and she is best seen as one of that eminent line of nature writers of whom Thoreau was the first and most famous. This means that she wrote of nature less as a scientist, observing, classifying, cataloguing (she did less of this than Thoreau), and more as a person determined to communicate personal experience. She wrote with his same sense of intimacy and oneness with other living things, plant and animal, and like him she continuously sought to discover the human relevance in objects and events in nature.

For the most part, nature was for her a place of beauty and harmony, a restorative source of health. Penny Baxter in *The Yearling* went to the scrub to live because his spirit had been bruised too often among men: "The peace of the vast aloof scrub had drawn him with the beneficence of its silence. Something in him was raw and tender. The touch of men was hurtful upon it, but the touch of the pines was healing. Making a living came harder there . . . but the clearing was peculiarly his own. The wild animals seemed less predatory to him than people he had known. The forays of bear and wolf and wildcat and panther on stock were understandable, which was more than he could say of human cruelties" [*Y*, 18]. This is a classic statement of the romantic doctrine that nature can heal the human spirit which has been hurt by life in cities, and one detects in it more than a hint of her own reasons for moving from Rochester to Cross Creek. Nature for her also has terror, as when Penny is struck by the rattlesnake, and an inscrutable violence and cruelty, as when the great storm destroys the Baxters' crops and floods the scrub country so that the wild creatures are drowned by the hundreds. Donald Culross Peattie, the naturalist, after reading *The Yearling* aloud to his two small sons, wrote to Marjorie complimenting her on the rigor and honesty of her depiction of nature: "I might add, since it is in my line, that while anyone can write about Nature, very few can stand up to Nature as you do. Few look at it as it is. People play with prettiness; they paint its colors; they read in it something that is not written there. You are a minute observer of Nature, a conscientious reporter, understanding and wise, and brave enough for it" [DCP to MKR January 28, 1940].

During her early years at the grove, because of the struggle against drought and frost and insects, she sometimes felt that she would be driven forth like so many other Yankees by the violence which she soon found was the other side to the beauty of this country. "The region is beautiful," she told Perkins in

1931, "but it is not pretty. It is like a beautiful woman capable of deep evil and a great treachery. Back of the lushness is something stark and sinister" [MKR to MEP March 31, 1931]. She had discovered from experience the extremes of wind and temperature which after weeks or months of idyllic mildness could bring sudden calamity to a farmer. Her early novelette, "Jacob's Ladder," she originally entitled "High Winds" because violent weather has so prominent a place in it—two hurricanes, a prolonged drought, and a rare Florida winter snowstorm within two years' elapsed time. The local Gainesville weekly *News* in reviewing the story was indignant at her depiction of the Florida climate, and accused her of not knowing her subject. Actually each of the episodes in the story was true enough, even if such spells of hard weather might not occur in such concentration. Marjorie, quite unrepentant, because she knew she was telling the truth, included in future stories similar episodes of natural violence or catastrophe.

Her predominant reaction to Florida was delight. Even after a desperate summer of fighting to keep the Mediterranean fruit fly out of her area, she was still so captivated by her chosen home that she could write:

The place is likely to drive us forth, clutching our pants about our naked waists . . . but if I leave it will be reluctantly with backward lookings, forever to be tormented with the Heimweh. *It would be easy to grow O'Brienish and tell why. The passionate, impassioning odor of ten acres of orange blossoms in the moonlight—a climate, aside from the insects, that is a constant sensual luxury—rivers that are startlingly Conradian, and as moving—deep hammock-lands, deep and dark with the magnificent gloom of magnolias, of bay trees, of live oaks—"the scrub," high pine lands sloping down to the Oklawaha valley—silvermullet leaping in the Withlacoochee—blue herons across green marsh grass, like Japanese panels—white egrets in full plumage—the track of a mother wildcat down your road, followed by the spoor of a whole litter of her kits—the inch-long sea-green frogs that sleep in the yellow trumpet flowers of the allamanda—oh, never mind. When one has paid a dollar and a half a piece for gardenias in New York City, to wear for half a day—and then regretted the extravagance—to find gardenias, under the name of cape jasmine, in full bloom in every nigger's door-yard, sums it up: the luxury of beauty made constantly available* [*MS fragment, "Cracker Florida*"].

The little citrus grove she bought at Cross Creek was irresistible to her precisely because of its remoteness—four miles off any paved road, between two great shallow lakes whose perimeters were still jungle. Living on a narrow spit of dry ground virtually surrounded by water or swamp for many square miles, she was ideally located to have a maximum exposure to a large amount and variety of Florida wildlife. The area is naturally attractive to birds, so that she was constantly aware of their passing in the skies, their rustle in the underbrush, their calling or their song. At the Creek she could feel the night air pulsating with the whine of insects and the singing of numberless frogs. She knew that under the broiling summer sun the marshy areas around Orange Lake were like a primordial cauldron literally bubbling and seething with a green biologic stew of new life. In the orange grove or in the hammock areas near her house she could walk under heavy, junglelike shade even on the brightest days, but elsewhere she was aware of a wide horizon as at the seacoast and of the continuous drama of the Florida sky, so that the fantastic cloud shapes and the intense high blue, the rain and wind, moonlight and darkness, sunrise and sunset, the whole swing and movement of the seasons were all an intimate part of her daily life.

Although she was sensitive to many facets of natural life, her interest seems to have run first to the world of plants, which she *understood*, for which she had a true feeling of sympathy and involvement as toward animate creatures. Of a magnolia tree outside her kitchen window she wrote:

I do not know the irreducible minimum of happiness for any other spirit than my own. It is impossible to be certain even of mine. Yet I believe that I know my tangible desideratum. It is a tree-top against a patch of sky. If I should lie crippled or long ill, or should have the quite conceivable misfortune to be clapped in jail, I could survive, I think, given this one token of the physi-

> *cal world. I know that I lived on one such in my first days at the Creek.*
>
> *The tree was a magnolia, taller than the tallest orange trees around it. There is no such thing in the world as an ugly tree, but the* magnolia grandiflora *has a unique perfection. No matter how crowded it may be, no matter how thickly holly and live oak and sweet gum may grow up around it, it develops with complete symmetry, so that one wonders whether character in all things, human as well as vegetable, may not be implicit. Neither is its development ruthless, achieved at the expense of its neighbors, for it is one of the few trees that may be allowed to stand in an orange grove, seeming to steal nothing from the expensively nourished citrus. The young of the tree is courteous, waiting for the parent to be done with life before presuming to take it over. There are never seedling magnolias under or near an old magnolia. When the tree at last dies, the young glossy sprouts appear from nowhere, exulting in the sun and air for which they may have waited a long hundred years* [CC, 28-29].

This is tree conceived in terms of personality, beauty described in terms of character; the passage might have been written by Thoreau or one of the other transcendentalists with ethical imagination. She shows a proper regard for physical truth in the accuracy of her observation: "The red seed cones are as fine as candles. They mature slowly from the top of the tree down, as a Christmas tree is lighted." But always the natural "fact" in her writing is given added dimensions of meaning because it is enveloped and permeated by her own personal involvement and commitment. She would have agreed with Thoreau's belief that "nature must be viewed humanly to be viewed at all," and that "a man has not seen a thing until he has *felt* it" [*Summer*, 43; *Winter*, 430 (February 23, 1860)].

The quickness with which she picked up names of the local plants is astonishing. Within a year of her coming she was referring in her notes with perfect ease and undeviating accuracy to gallberry, ti-ti, hackberry, trifoliata, spider-wort, coffee-weed, jessamine, sparkleberry, and dozens of other plants which she could never have known in the North. One has the sense that she never passed an unfamiliar plant without making its acquaintance, and that once identified it became a permanent friend of whose existence she was always aware. She knew plant life by taste and smell as well as by sight, by color and by texture, by leaf, bark, and flower, in green season and brown. In *South Moon Under* she describes the boy Lant walking in the hammock land near the Oklawaha River: "The April sunlight, so fiercely strident in the open, was defeated by the dark hammock and filtered in thin patches to the ground. The earth here was cool. Ferns were moist and sweet-scented and fungus sprouted, sometimes in alabaster sprays like unearthly flowers. He broke one off; smelled of its loamy must; touched his tongue to the stem, splintered like crystal; remembered old man Paine's warning against poisonous herbs and threw it down" [*SMU*, 72]. This is plant life apprehended in three dimensions of sense impression, and one detects in it a reflection of her own experience.

A flower garden was as staple a necessity to her happiness as food and, in the black loam outside her kitchen, side by side with rows of lettuce or collard greens, she grew the common cut flowers all year round except for a few weeks of frost during the winter. When she could afford it, or had a grove hand with a green thumb like the Negro Samson, she had roses. During most seasons she had wild flowers—magnolia or bay, blue iris or yellow lotus, which grew by profuse acres in the swampy areas near-by.

Of all creatures in the animal world, birds held the steadiest fascination for her. She even said, more than half seriously, that if reincarnation was true and she could choose the creature she would be in another life, she would choose to be a redbird, because he enjoys life so thoroughly, and because he is so beautiful and sings so sweetly. She was continuously alert to the multifarious bird life around her at the grove, particularly at the feeding station just outside her back door, which she looked on as a source of daily drama. She had a similar interest in, but less opportunity to observe closely, the wilder birds of the lake, marsh, and forest, but even these she knew at least by sight, watching with the same alert interest and habit of identification she used with plants. The sharpness of her observation is illustrated by her comments on the differences in bird flight, originally set down as notes shortly after her arrival at the Creek, then later revised and included in *Cross Creek:*

Something about the eagle's circling is more purposeful than that of the buzzard. The great wings lie in a straighter line on the air, without so much of uptilted curve.

. . . the hummingbird reveals himself by his swinging arcs. It is as though he were suspended on an invisible wire and swung only to its limits. The woodpeckers, too, seem to be motivated by puppets' strings and drop jerkily a few feet down a tree-trunk, only to be jerked back up again. When they fly, they open and close their wings and propel themselves like a boy with one foot on a scooter.

The little ground doves fly as though uncertain of themselves, like apprentice birds learning the business. They take off with a whirring of tiny rose-lined wings, achieving the safety of the crepe myrtle with a spasmodic effort. I perpetually expect them to miss the bough they have aimed for and topple indignantly to the ground, for they flutter nervously as they land. . . . A covey of quail explodes like a pan of popcorn popping and I can recognize the spasmic scattering far across the grove. . . .

The most engaging of bird flights to my notion is that of the red-birds. They seem to take life very lightly and in motion they give an effect of haphazard gayety. They seem not to fly of their own volition, but, scatterbrained, to be tossed from tree to tree like wind-blown leaves [CC, 271-72].

One unusual sequence in *Cross Creek* describes a flock of Mallard ducks which she raised from eggs and then released to full freedom when they were grown. Instead of flying off to Orange Lake only a few hundred yards away, and thus back to the wild state, they stayed on for years, content to use the orange grove as their home base. She was attracted not only by their beauty, but by their pure delight in living: "My . . . Mallards possess to the highest degree of any creatures I know, animal or human, an acutely conscious *joie de vivre*. A dog knows when he is having a good time. But his fun derives from a definite objective, a walk, a ride, a hunt, a swim. The Mallards awaken with the first tinge of light, shake their wings, and give voice to their delight as plainly as though they shouted, 'Hah! Another day of good living!' " [*CC*, 251]. Her account caught the personality of these creatures so vividly that it drew a letter of praise from the great ornithologist, Frank M. Chapman, curator of the Museum of Natural History in New York. "It's a pity," he wrote, "you have never gotten 'round to other birds to crown them with the immortality of your young Mallards. That kind of bird book remains to be written."

Other more strictly domestic creatures were always an important part of Marjorie's life at Cross Creek. Included with the grove at the time of purchase were a pair of mules and a flock of two hundred chickens, which she soon disposed of except for a few to provide eggs for the house, but for novelty she bought a number of guinea fowl and the game chickens which on occasion she hunted for the table with a .22 rifle. She also acquired the first of a long succession of cows, calves, heifers, and scrub bulls. The pair of mules which came with the place proved useful for working the grove during her first years there, but the cattle were not strictly necessary and soon showed themselves to be a continual nuisance, breaking out of fences, requiring constant care and expense. Marjorie's experience with such larger animals had been limited to sporadic association during summer vacations when she was a girl; she did not even know how to milk a cow before coming to Florida, and whenever possible she left the care of the livestock to the Rawlings men while they were on the place or to hired help during the years she lived there alone. She kept the cows partly because of the copious milk and cream they made available to her kitchen, but she could have obtained this just as well from near neighbors. The main reason she put up with them seems to have been because they satisfied her romantic ideal of what a farm should be and gave her a pleasant sense of self-sufficiency, as a city dweller might keep shelves of homemade jellies and preserves in the basement, more for the glow of feeling independent from the supermarket than from any actual need.

Her Florida life always contained pets of many sorts, but most importantly the muscular heartiness and affection of bird dogs, first Pat and then Moe, pointers whom she loved as members of the family. There was also Racket, her pet raccoon, whose winsome viciousness found its way into both *Cross Creek* and *The Yearling*, and in her later years Siamese cats like Uki, whose expensive elegance fitly symbolized her withdrawal from the pastoral adventure at Cross Creek to St. Augustine and predominantly city ways.

The animal lore which makes up so important a part of the local color in her books is the more impressive when one recalls that virtually all of this was knowledge acquired after her coming to Cross Creek. To record with warmth and humor her experience with domestic animals may not seem remarkable, but to learn so much of the ways of truly wild creatures—bear, deer, wildcat—is a substantial achievement. Most of her knowledge of wildlife came from two sources, her prolonged visits in the Big Scrub with the Fiddias and the Longs, and her conversations with many persons experienced in nature and hunting lore including the old hunter Barney Dillard, and her friends Fred Tompkins, Chet Crosby, and Dessie Smith. If her own prowess as huntress was modest and her actual firsthand experience with hunting limited, she nevertheless lived enough of the life so that everything she heard from other sources had vivid and concrete reality in her mind, and she seems never to have forgotten anything she ever saw or heard talked about. The country itself she knew so well from personal experience that when she tells of Penny and Jody Baxter tracking Ol' Slewfoot through the scrub in *The Yearling* the particulars of terrain are utterly faithful. But most details of bear life which are welded seamlessly into the account came to her as anecdotes from Barney Dillard or Cal Long, who had had the actual experiences. The passage where Penny Baxter tells his son about bears eating fire-plant as a spring tonic provides a good example:

"Many's the time I've seed a bear feedin' on the fire-plant in the moonlight. He'll snort and shuffle, and splash and grunt. He'll rip them leaves offen the stems and cram 'em in his ugly ol' mouth like a person. Then he'll nose along and chaw, like a dog

chawin' grass. And the night-birds cryin' over him, and the bull-frogs hollerin' like nigger-dogs, and the Mallards callin' 'Snake! Snake! Snake!' and the drops o' water on the leaves o' the fire-plant shinin' bright and red as a bull-bat's eyes—" [*Y*, 34].

In such passages the dialect, the very intonation, of the voice, as well as the most convincing details of the experience have been caught. She had actually had almost no personal experience of bears, but her transcription is so faithful that it gives the impression of an eyewitness account. The hundreds of details of hunting lore so liberally seeded through her books are to an important degree this kind of second-hand knowledge imaginatively re-created. Occasionally some unusual wilderness experience which she had heard from her old hunter friends is modified as she tells it. One of the most memorable of such episodes is the dance of the whooping cranes which Penny and Jody Baxter observe in a marsh at sunset:

The cranes were dancing a cotillion as surely as it was danced at Volusia. Two stood apart, erect and white, making a strange music that was part cry and part singing. The rhythm was irregular, like the dance. The other birds were in a circle. In the heart of the circle, several moved counter-clock-wise. The musicians made their music. The dancers raised their wings and lifted their feet, first one and then the other. They sunk their heads deep in their snowy breasts, lifted them and sunk again. They moved soundlessly, part awkwardness, part grace. The dance was solemn. Wings fluttered, rising and falling like outstretched arms. The outer circle shuffled around and around. The group in the center attained a slow frenzy.

. . . The evening breeze moved across the sawgrass. It bowed and fluttered. The water rippled. The setting sun lay rosy on the white bodies. Magic birds were dancing in a mystic marsh. The grass swayed with them, and the shallow water, and the earth fluttered under them. The earth was dancing with the cranes, and the low sun, and the wind and sky.

Jody found his own arms lifting and falling with his breath, as the cranes' wings lifted [*Y*, 94-95].

In a passage of this sort, the raw materials of experience furnished by Barney Dillard or Cal Long have undergone a major transformation into a kind of rhapsodic tone poem, in which all traces of dialect are gone and the words and almost the conception itself are the author's own.

After *The Yearling* was published, she wrote to Perkins, "I know you think I put too much emphasis on the importance of fact in fiction, but it seems to me that this type of work is not valid if the nature lore behind it is not true in every detail." She confessed that for a time after the book's appearance she half held her breath wondering if the hunting sequences would seem convincing to the men who really knew. Then she got a letter one day from one of her hunting cronies who told her that reading the book had made him so homesick for the scrub and for the hunting that he was tempted to throw up his job and go back to live there. The Juniper Club, a group of Louisville businessmen who owned a hunting lodge near Silver Glen Springs and a large tract of the scrub as a hunting ground, wrote her enthusiastically and offered to make her an honorary member of the club. There was no doubt that the nature lore and the hunting scenes rang true.

Most persons in Florida, particularly those in cities, live from year to year without seeing any reptile larger than a chameleon, but at Cross Creek Marjorie lived in real snake territory. The marshes of Lake Lochloosa and Orange Lake contained uncounted hundreds of moccasins, and the palmetto thickets and the scrubby pasture across the road to the east of her property held more than their share of rattlesnakes, and all the other lesser varieties in that half-wild area were equally numerous. A number of her own experiences with snakes are treated at some length in a chapter in *Cross Creek* entitled "The Ancient Enmity," which she was careful to preface with the statement that she had discovered that snakes were not nearly so omnipresent in Florida as myth would have it. Nevertheless she had more encounters than most people.

She had unusual physical courage, learned over the years by facing down her physical fears one at a time, but she freely admitted to a deep, unreasoning phobia against snakes. Some of this dread moderated from the sheer frequency with which she encountered the ancient enemy in her daily routine at the Creek, and she lost another portion of it on the two-day snake hunt down in the Everglades near Okeechobee with Ross Allen, a professional herpetologist from Silver Springs. But she never entirely got over her fear, because she had experiences from time to time which shocked it back to life. She tells of snapping on the bathroom light one evening to discover a big moccasin coiled in the toilet bowl, of opening a kitchen cabinet to reach for a plate only to look into the eyes of an oak snake a few inches from her face. A quiet afternoon on Orange Lake when she was fishing with Julia Scribner and Chet Crosby all at once became a time of horror, when moccasins, which usually mind their own business, began for some mysterious reason to slither up out of the water into the boat. Chet would beat one out with an oar only to have another appear over a different gunwale—over and over again as in a nightmare, until they were finally able to move the boat to another area. Her early notes, which cover multifarious aspects of the country and its creatures, contain very few references to snakes, nor are they prominent in her fiction. There is an unfinished story called "Snake Bit," parts of which in modified form were worked into "Cracker Chidlings," and there is the terrible scene in *The Yearling* describing Penny's agony with the rattlesnake, but on the whole she develops very few incidents involving snakes.

With alligators it is quite otherwise. She loved to write about "those preposterous creatures," as she called them, and gave them important episodes in *South Moon Under*, *The Yearling*, and *Cross Creek*, as well as feature treatment in the short story entitled "Alligators." There is no other fictional treatment of these animals containing the same combination of sharp realistic fact with the wild comic exaggeration of the frontier tall tale. In addition to the stories from Fred Tompkins, she had had personal experience of them on Orange Lake and in her prowling on the Oklawaha with Leonard Fiddia. She knew exactly the orange, unwinking glare of a 'gator's eyes picked out by searchlight at night, and she had smelled the heavy fishy musk of a 'gator cave;

she had seen them shot and harpooned. Oddly, she was not in the least intimidated by their alien and fearsome qualities, so that most of her accounts of them are written with a bemused detachment.

She had a particular fascination for the stories she had heard from Cal Long about a wolf pack which ran in the scrub in the 1870's, and tried to work this material into *South Moon Under*, but it never seemed to fit and she set it aside until she found a proper place for it in *The Yearling*. There Jody and Penny catch a glimpse of a pack of thirty, gaunt, gray figures as they leap into the undergrowth after killing one of the Baxter's heifers. In real life this was one of the last wolf packs east of the Mississippi River, which Cal Long's father had actually seen, and in real life as in the book, the pack was reduced by bait poisoned by strychnine, then the remnant hunted down from horseback and shot.

Of all the sequences in her books involving wild creatures, no other has held the steady appeal of her depiction of Jody's pet fawn, Flag. The depth and purity of Jody's love for his pet, the innocent softness and graceful beauty of the young deer, have caught at the hearts of young and old readers alike. The idea for the pet fawn came to Marjorie from Cal Long, whose brother Mel had had such a pet when they were boys living at Pat's Island. She had already learned a great deal about deer behavior from her first stay in the scrub with the Fiddias, and she had much more from the Longs and from Barney Dillard. She knew from sources of this kind that a fawn would stay where its mother left it, that a doe fawn's spots are scattered and a buck fawn's are in a straight line, that a fawn would follow a person who had carried it. But many other details of the ways of young deer she acquired first hand from observing the deer which were kept penned at Silver Glen Springs—the kind of intimate detail she had to know in order to write such scenes as the one where Jody gives the fawn his first feeding:

He poured milk into a small gourd. He held it out to the fawn. It butted it suddenly, smelling the milk. He saved it precariously from spilling over the floor. He led the fawn outside to the yard and began again. It could make nothing of the milk in the gourd.

He dipped his fingers in the milk and thrust them into the fawn's soft wet mouth. It sucked greedily. When he withdrew them, it bleated frantically and butted him. He dipped his fingers again and as the fawn sucked, he lowered them slowly into the milk. The fawn blew and sucked and snorted. It stamped its small hooves impatiently. As long as he held his fingers below the level of the milk, the fawn was content. It closed its eyes dreamily. It was ecstasy to feel its tongue against his hand. Its small tail flicked back and forth. The last of the milk vanished in a swirl of foam and gurgling. The fawn bleated and butted but its frenzy was appeased [*Y*, 173-74].

Most of the details of the fawn's behavior as a pet in the home, such as his ability to open the shoe-string latch and come in at any time, she had from Cal Long, and from the same source came the climactic pathos in Jody's love for his pet, the necessity for its being destroyed because as it grew it leaped the highest fences and ate the young crops—this was also a true part of the original story of the pet deer in the Long family. A remarkable feature of her nature-writing is that she achieves so uniform a tone of authenticity that one is seldom aware which elements come to her from firsthand experience and which from second-hand report.

The range of her interest in natural phenomena is unusual. She is concerned not only with the largest considerations of climate, weather, changing season, the general aspects of the countryside, and the habits of animals; she is also concerned with the minute. She knew that Spanish moss has tiny, almost invisible rose-colored blossoms in early spring, and she looked with intent interest at such creatures as ants, chameleons, and the small green rain frogs: "If frogs an inch long have never been carved in apple-green jade, they should be. Nothing else could repeat the jewel-like perfection of this diminutive species. Their eyes are tiny moonstones. . . .

"They are a celestial breed of frogs and in season are found in apartments suitable to reincarnated Chinese emperors—large yellow allamanda blossoms" [*CC*, 145]. Like the transcendentalists whom she resembles so sharply in some ways, she often was willing to let her mind flow out from natural fact to an imaginative speculation which links the most unlikely categories and comes to rest ultimately in a moral observation: "There is an uncanny resemblance between the frogs and the buds of the allamanda. Until they open, the buds are precisely the size and shape of the frogs. Until well along into yellow prematurity, they are even the same shade of green. They have the same snub nose, the same little bulges of two eyes. It is easy to imagine that the more royal frogs are born in the allamanda blossoms, giving the buds their shape. It seems as though there must be a mystic affinity between the flower and its inhabitant. If I were a theosophist, I should certainly revere the tiny frogs as the living shape of Chinese aristocrats, who, even in an enforced humility of form, maintain an archaic arrogance" [*CC*, 146].

Thoreau called himself a self-appointed inspector of snowstorms and rainstorms, a surveyor of forest paths and all across-lots routes. Marjorie had no snowstorms to keep track of, but she was a faithful inspector of the weather and the seasons as they rolled through Cross Creek, and all of her longer works reflect this continuous awareness of the seasonal variations. She loved them all—even at times the oppressive heat of late August. In romantic fashion she reveled in the thunderstorms of midsummer and even, with a proper touch of awe, in the northeasters and the great hurricane storms of autumn. In midwinter, when the destructive cold fronts blew in with icy winds from the Great Plains, she was moved by the beauty of the cold nights even though her grove might be threatened with destruction.

An important part of Marjorie's personal philosophy and religious attitudes centered on her attitude toward nature. She was as much of a pantheist as Whitman and felt a strong sense of identification with the whole process of life. Her belief that all men are born with an attachment to the earth led her to a conviction that the closer one's intimacy with the natural world, the fuller and happier would be his life. When she moved to Cross

Creek she took with her a Scottish terrier, Dinghy, and a cat named Jib. Dinghy, she said, hated the Florida backwoods from the first sandspur under his tail and was miserable until he was taken back to the city; the cat loved the jungle from the first moment and throve on the wildness. She makes it clear that her own reaction was like the cat's, and she implies that the cat was somehow good because he loved the wildness of the Creek, the dog somehow bad because he hated it and preferred cities. All the protagonists of her major stories exhibit a similar quiet but passionate affinity for unspoiled nature. One reason Lant liked moonshining as an occupation was because it gave him the chance to spend long hours of uninterrupted communion with the jungle: "He liked the intimacy with the hammock. Its life washed over him and he became a part of it. The scrub yonder sent its furred and feathered inhabitants past him to eat and drink, and he and the scrub were one" [*SMU*, 224]. In *Cross Creek* she tells of walking alone one day in the hammock land near Orange Lake and encountering a wild sow giving birth to her litter under a magnolia tree, then she makes this unusual statement: "The jungle hammock breathed. Life went through the moss-hung forest, the swamp, the cypresses, through the wild sow and her young, through me, in its continuous chain. We were all one with the silent pulsing. This was the thing that was important, the cycle of life, with birth and death merging one into the other in an imperceptible twilight and an insubstantial dawn" [*CC*, 39].

This was the way she conceived of God—as a great Life running through all things which was made up of individual lives as the ocean is made up of individual drops of water. In *The Sojourner* her representative man, Ase Linden, actually uses this Emersonian metaphor as he speculates about the nature of God. Her own contemplation of God always started with the natural world around her, then like Ase Linden she almost always raised her eyes to the heavens and let her mind range through space to that other dimension of her pantheism which she called "cosmic consciousness." The passage about the wild sow concludes by shifting into this cosmic dimension: "The universe breathed, and the world inside it breathed the same breath. This was the cosmic life, with suns and moons to make it lovely. It was important only to keep close enough to the pulse to feel its rhythm, to be comforted by its steadiness, to know that Life is vital, and one's own minute living a torn fragment of the larger cloth" (*CC*, 39). Death, according to this view, and she represents it thus at the end of *The Sojourner*, is simply the release of the spirit from its earthly bonds so that it can continue its migration out into the cosmos, eventually perhaps to break completely free of all restraints and merge in oneness with the larger Life—another concept she shares with Whitman and the transcendentalists.

Mixed with Marjorie's cosmic optimism was a contradictory streak of earthy realism. In addition to her own painful experience with nature's harshness, she had imbibed enough of modern evolutionary thought so that she sometimes pictured life in nature as an unceasing predatory warfare. The boy Jody learns in *The Yearling* that Baxter's Island is a fortress in the scrub, an island of plenty in a hungry sea, maintained only by constant vigil and struggle, maintained at the price of sacrificing the creature he loved most in the world. Outside in the scrub the animals preyed ceaselessly upon one another, and when they could they made incursions on the clearing, as he and his father made forays outside for the flesh of the deer and the fur of the wildcat. Though not much given to conscious symbolism, Marjorie creates a powerful symbolic picture of man as a puny helpless creature in a darkly hostile nature in the scene where Penny is struck by the rattlesnake. Jody is sent by his father to get help from the Forresters and as he makes his way alone in the dark through the wilderness he hears a snarl from the bushes beside him and smells a strong animal musk in the air. But he never catches sight of what creature it is and must plod on in the blackness filled with panic and terror of the unseen. Now a quick thunderstorm rises and sweeps through the scrub and, to keep his clothes from getting drenched, Jody strips off shirt and breeches, rolls them into a bundle, and pushes on through the heavy wind and pelting rain. "He was alone and naked in an unfriendly world; lost and forgotten in the storm and darkness. Something ran behind him and ahead of him. It stalked the scrub like a panther. It was vast and formless and it was his enemy. Ol' Death was loose in the scrub" [*Y*, 153].

In a later section of the book, after the great northeaster has blown for seven days, drowning the scrub and destroying the crops which are the Baxters' main means of survival, Penny still has enough spirit to quip wryly that the Baxters have had it easier than Job in their afflictions, since none of them has had boils as yet. His wife snaps back, "Find the good in it, that's right." Penny's reply expresses Marjorie's own somber understanding of the human condition: "They ain't no good in it. Lest it is to remind a man to be humble, for there's nary thing on earth he kin call his own."

But even though Marjorie's Florida wilderness has its great flood and its snake, it remains for her a kind of Eden, and her writing about it is lyric rather than prophetic. It is mainly a pleasant wilderness, more idyllic than evil, and one finds himself using the words sylvan, bucolic, pastoral—rather than brute, savage, untamed—to describe it. Hers is a jungle with most of its fangs drawn; the predators—wolf, bear, or aborigine—have either been eliminated or are rapidly being destroyed, so as to leave predominantly a wilderness of flora, along with the comfortable lesser fauna to give one the thrill of encounter with the brute. One seldom meets the categorically savage and primordial, which were so important to Faulkner, the hot rank stench of a great bear rearing over one with paws outstretched, the great buck whom one salutes with "Oleh! Grandfather, Chief!" Her wilderness also contains or borders upon plowed fields, and her attitudes toward wild nature are mixed with agrarian or pastoral attitudes, which also spring from an essentially mystic insistence upon a holy harmony between man and earth. The place to examine these is on her Cracker Frontier, the other major facet of her regionalism.

5

The Cracker Frontier

NO ONE KNOWS for sure where the word "cracker" came from as a name for the white settlers of inland Florida. Some claim that it is based on the practice of these people of cracking dry corn to make the meal and grits so important to their diet; some claim that it refers to their skill in cracking the great whips they used to drive their oxen and cattle; still others claim that it comes from a Spanish word *cuacaros* meaning "Quakers." Whatever its origin, "cracker" now has not one but several common usages. City folk in Florida use it to refer (often in a slurring sense) to any poor white Floridian, particularly if he lives in the country. In another usage "cracker" simply refers with no coloring of favor or disfavor to any Floridian, rich or poor, country or city, as persons from Indiana are Hoosiers or persons from North Carolina are Tarheels. But as Marjorie Rawlings used the word, and as it will be used here, it refers to the white country folk, the "natives" who were living in her part of rural central Florida when she came.

There is no scholarly study of these people. As it turns out, Marjorie's account is the fullest as it is the most readable and colorful. The best evidence suggests that the crackers were originally poor backwoodsman farmers of English and Scotch-Irish stock, chiefly from Georgia and the Carolinas, who settled in central Florida in the years just before and just after the Civil War. West Florida had already been settled as early as the 1830's by slave-holding planters of quite different origins, as had the seacoast areas near Fernandina and the St. Johns valley as far south as Lake George.

A distinguishing feature of these people was poverty; they were poor when they came into the state and on the whole they remained poor. As an offshoot of the people who settled the highlands of Appalachia, they were related to the southern poor-whites who became the hillbillies of fiction, stage, and comic-strip, but the cracker as depicted by Marjorie has little in common with the slack-mouthed degenerates who inhabited Tobacco Road, or with such comic grotesques as Snuffy Smith or L'il Abner. Her view of the Florida poor-white was stated explicitly in a talk entitled "The Invisible Florida" which she gave at Florida Southern College in 1935, after she had been writing about these people for nearly seven years. She said she had deliberately excluded many Floridas from her writing, the Florida of business, of agriculture, of tourists, of sophisticated play. She declared her concern for another Florida with a past and present but very little future, which must decrease as the others increase. "It is the Florida where a man can still make a living with an axe and a gun . . . the Florida of the hammock, the piney-woods, the great silent scrub. . . . This is the Florida, wild and natural, that I'm calling 'the invisible Florida.' Not because it's remote or inaccessible and can't be seen, because there it is, a physical sight plain to anyone. But it is invisible because its beauty must be seen with the spiritual eye as well as the physical eye. . . . I've longed to re-create, to make visible, this invisible beauty. . . . The true Florida crackers are almost gone, and I regret it because they are an integral part of their background, and beautiful in their repose, their dignity, their self-respect. Life has never been easy for them, but it has a distinct graciousness."

Her attitude was remarkable in its insistence that these people were "beautiful," a view shared by so few others that she felt a kind of missionary drive to make others see the beauty she saw. "You must have seen," she continued in her talk, "some withered old woman in a gray and white percale dress, standing in the doorway of an unpainted pine shack under a live oak or a magnolia, and felt that she was a strong and lovely part of a sturdy, an admirable and difficult life." The chances are that not very many persons in her audience would have had such pleasant thoughts at all, but conditioned by an extensive literature which depicted the poor-white as slovenly and degenerate, would have felt something quite different.

Other writers have looked on the same Florida that was the center of Marjorie's interest and have seen very little that was gracious or beautiful. Edwin Granberry in *Strangers and Lovers* [New York, 1930] and Theodore Pratt in *Big Blow* [Boston, 1936], both contemporaries of Marjorie, represented the Florida cracker in the most uncomplimentary terms, seeing mainly lawlessness, backwardness, and moral degeneracy. Many of the post-Civil War guide books and travel books mention the crackers, but always unsympathetically, as in the following account by George Barbour which describes the "natives" in the Brooksville area in the 1870's: "The only human beings living anywhere along the road [were] four or five families of Florida natives, the genuine, unadulterated 'cracker'—the clay-eating, gaunt, pale, tallowy, leather-skinned sort—stupid, stolid, staring eyes, dead and lusterless; unkempt hair, generally tow-colored; and such a shiftless, slouching manner! simply white savages—or living white mummies would, perhaps, better indicate their dead-alive looks and actions. . . . Stupid and shiftless, yet shy and vindictive, they are a block in the pathway of civilization, settlement, and enterprise wherever they exist. Fortunately, however, they are very few and rapidly decreasing in numbers, for they cannot exist near civilized settlements." [*Florida for Tourists, Invalids, and Settlers*, Facsimile Reproduction, 1882 ed., Gainesville, Fla., 54].

In such accounts, the crackers are looked upon as an alien and inferior race, with something like the scorn and condescension of the British pukka sahib toward the "colonials." Marjorie's account is unique, not only because it is the fullest, but because it is the only one written from the inside, from an intimate contact with the way of life and a personal knowledge of the people. Her concern to present this people and their way of life—including the moonshining and the poaching of deer out of season—as something beautiful was so strong that she felt she had failed as an artist when anyone read her books and was left with a sense of ugliness. "I'm always horrified," she told her Lakeland audience, "when someone, as happens now and then, speaks of the characters in *South Moon Under* as degenerate and compares them with the hideous characters of such a book as *Tobacco Road*. It seems painfully bigoted to attribute degeneracy to anyone living a simpler more difficult life than one's own—to drink moonshine and yet condemn moonshining."

Like so many other aspects of her writing, her conception of these people is keyed to her theory about adjustment to environment. She recognized that the true crackers lived in unusually close harmony with their wild background, and this she felt must have an important molding influence on their character. They could not possibly be like the inhabitants of *Tobacco Road* because their environment was so totally different. "I had met only two or three of the neighboring crackers," she told Stephen Vincent Benét in 1941, "when I realized that isolation had done something to these people. Rather . . . civilization had remained too remote . . . to take from them something vital. They have a primal quality against their background of jungle hammock . . . against the tremendous silence of the scrub country. The only ingredients of their lives are the elemental things" [*New York Herald Tribune Books*, February 2, 1941].

An unpublished manuscript entitled "Cracker Florida," dating from the summer of 1930 and apparently intended originally as a feature news story, preserves her first attempt to make a comprehensive statement about the cracker. This first conception was never changed, only elaborated and extended in the subsequent books based on Florida material:

Who are the Florida Crackers? They are a people without a history, as Florida is a state with wide gaps in its genealogy. They are folk whose mothers and fathers or grandmothers and grandfathers migrated down from Georgia farms and Carolina plantations. They have a background of small plantings of rice and cotton and tobacco. An independent people, poor as long as they can remember, competing with the Negro for labor, forced by him to work for lower wages than can be decently lived on. Pride, as well as necessity, forces them into fishing, trapping, and hunting. Many of them come from they know not where, offspring of fugitives from justice who hid themselves in the last century in the Florida scrub and hammocks.

Georgia seems the mother of the cracker Florida. She overflowed into the more southern state, sending out small, poor farmers in search of the ever-kinder clime, the ever-readier soil. She has sent them with her speech, her Brunswick stew, her cane syrup, and her hate of the Negro.

The Cracker fits into his environment like jack pine. The local Negro, in comparison, is a little alien. The Negro settlements for the most part are sun-baked excrescences, visible for miles in open, tree-less areas or along cleared roads. A Cracker house is come on suddenly, its gray weather-beaten frame emerging from the moss that curtains it, draped from over-hanging live oaks, magnolias and sweet gum trees. There is a crepe myrtle at the door, blossoming pink, white or lavender in Biblical profusion. An oleander is scraggly at the side. Clumps of allamanda, of sprawling lantana, of spider lilies, whose opening fistules of buds are called, and indeed resemble, "drowned men's fingers," spot the sandy yard, bare of grass. Green grass to the Cracker is an affectation, a sophistication, which he despises. He prefers the swept sand, raking it daily free, if he is energetic, of live oak leaves and palmetto fronds. A clump of dwarf bamboo forms a wind-break for a shed, where a mule drowses in the special apathy peculiar to mules and Negroes. A chinaberry tree invariably shades the outhouse.

The house is without screens and often without doors in the door frames or panes in the windows. There are broad porches front and back, and if the house is of any size or pretensions, there is a breezeway. The Cracker complains good-humoredly, "The mosquitoes like to eat us up this summer," but aside from sleeping under a mosquito bar, he makes no effort to exclude them. The building may be set on posts of cypress or palmetto, leaving sufficient area for the half-wild, razor-back hogs to root beneath. . . .

The Cracker with energy grows a garden, if his soil is rich enough to "make" crops, of his favorite vegetables: cow-peas, collard greens, cabbages. With or without energy, he has a patch of sweet potatoes and his wife grows a sweet potato vine in a homemade pine needle basket, for the decoration of the dining room.

He does not say, "I make a living at so-and-so." He says, "I depend on my bean crop for my pork and grits." Pork and grits constitute the chief Cracker sustenance. The pork is razor-back, inches deep in fat, and incredibly sweet and succulent. Grits are fine-ground hominy, cooked to a porridge, eaten only when swimming in pork gravy or syrup, or by the upper-class Crackers with cows, in butter. With a slab of saffron cornbread, this is a meal—any meal. Dinner is cooked hot at noon. A cloth is thrown over the table containing the remains which, eaten at random during the evening, constitute supper. Rancid butter-milk is fancied, but sweet milk goes to the chickens. Coffee is more than half chicory. The complexion color of the Cracker . . . is not the healthy tan one would expect of a people much in the sun, but a greenish-gray quite corpselike. The children in particular are subject to "risin's," immense boils, which do not appear to affect their general health. The race is lean, above the average in height, and aside from "risin's" and "chills and fever," is hardy with gaunt, hound-like strength. Even the middle-aged women are long and lean. There is hardly a protruding stomach, aside from a pregnant one, nor a forty-eight-inch bust, in Alachua County.

Because of the threat of the Mediterranean fruit fly, which could have wiped out her investment overnight and driven her off the land and back to the city, she was impressed by the cracker's relative immunity to such disasters. "The diet of the race is strictly indigenous. The fruit fly could sweep the state, laying waste all of the one hundred and seventy-two fruits and vegetables that are its hosts, and the Cracker could subsist, as he has always done, on the completely immune pork and grits and 'greens.' Folk of other food habits, in this contingency, that is not at all impossible, would simply have to get out, leaving the state to its natural inhabitants—the Crackers and the bugs. . . . I seem to speak as one who dislikes both Crackers and the interior. On the contrary, I have found more likable and entertaining characters here than in the last two cities of my dwelling."

The cracker as she saw him was no dull-witted peasant but intelligent and sensitive to beauty. "Aesthetically, he is far above the farmer of the east, northeast or middle west, the only farmer I know. This may be because he is not solely a grubber of the soil. He hunts and fishes more than he farms, and has the breadth of mind of the man conversant with lakes, rivers, forests and jungles. . . . The women and children are shy and reticent, but the men are frank and receptive to Yankee advances. They look the stranger straight in the eye, speaking without the furtiveness of the Yankee yokel. They are 'moughty sartin' not to give you information that may be to your advantage and their harm, but there is no undue suspicion of you. The moonshiner, the illicit trapper, hunter or fisherman, makes sure of your disinterestedness. Once he decides to trust you, he is willing to discuss the details of his business with you with an ingrained enjoyment of good conversation."

The way of life of Marjorie's cracker friends near Cross Creek had already begun to be warped toward civilization by the highway, the school bus, electric power, and the radio, but through them she was introduced to the Fiddia family and to others living in the scrub where isolation had preserved the older ways in purer form. Just as remoteness and inaccessibility had served to suspend change in some parts of the southern highlands, the dense wilderness of the scrub had acted as a barrier to the spread of settlement, so that those few families who chose to do so could live there in an island of the past protected by a wall of isolation which they willingly drew around themselves. Because of her Cross Creek friends, Marjorie was permitted to step behind the wall, and what was much more remarkable, was permitted to remain there and live for weeks enjoying the open confidence and friendship of the people. Not everyone could have done that. She made no secret of the fact that she was a writer gathering material for a book, and she asked questions and took notes quite openly, but it was part of her gift that she did so in such a way as to inspire the friendliest kind of acceptance and cooperation. Apparently they sensed her genuine approval for their way of life, which she entered into with such enthusiasm that she found herself losing some of her civilized perspective.

One reason for Marjorie's own missionary zeal toward the beauty of the cracker world and one reason for her choice of the phrase "The Invisible Florida" to refer to that world is that for a time the beauty had been invisible to her own eyes. In "Cracker Chidlings," which was written largely from notes gathered very early before she knew these people as friends, she is obviously the big-city reporter exhibiting picturesque natives for the amusement of other city-dwellers, making much of shiftlessness, drunkenness, and backwoods cuckoldry. In one sketch she describes a cracker, whom she calls 'Shiner Tim, in terms that make him sound like one of the degenerate Scraggs boys from L'il Abner: "His protection against the sheriff and his deputies is only his readiness to use his shotgun at the first sight of them. They respect the fact. He has killed and will kill again. He has the eye of a killer, dispassionate, disinterested, the eyelids heavy as a snake's. He has a trick of swaying his head from side to side like a moccasin weaving. He drinks his own raw liquor by the cupful, like water. He is never entirely sober but certainly never entirely drunk" [*Cr Ch*, 129]. This passage, written when she had seen the man and heard talk about him, but did not know him, almost certainly refers to the same Leonard Fiddia on whom she later based the highly sympathetic Lant of *South Moon Under*, and a large part of this account seems to be a stereotype superimposed upon scant knowledge of the man. There is no evidence that Leonard was a killer, either to protect his still or for any other reason, or that he had any of the other sinister qualities attributed to him here. 'Shiner Tim is the subject of another short story, "A Plumb Clare Conscience," written shortly after this, only now there is none of the condescension of the city-woman toward the hicks, and no straining for sensation. She is already inside the cracker world looking out upon it with their eyes, a confidante and trusted member of the inner circle of friends to whom 'Shiner Tim tells the tale of an extraordinary escape from the revenuers. In this story Tim is an engaging young man full of warmth and humor, who tells with self-effacing wit a tale of ingenuity and heroic physical endurance in escaping from agents who surprise him at his still.

So it was not an exploiter but a "believer," one already converted to the cracker viewpoint, who late in August of 1931 crossed the Oklawaha River into the scrub near Eureka and turned north up the small dirt road running along the river toward the Fiddia house. This is important because it determined in large measure what she was able to see. The way of life of the world she entered had only in some respects been arrested at the late frontier stage. The cracker families in the scrub were of course in touch with the twentieth century in many ways—Leonard Fiddia drove a battered Model-T Ford, and everyone in the scrub had access to modern gadgetry through the mail-order catalog, though this resource was limited by their severely limited cash income. The life was elemental in its closeness to wild nature and in the profound and timeless sense of being a severe struggle for existence with most of the "advantages" of industrial civilization lacking. The isolation itself was important and was made deeper by the lack of electricity and by the very few and very poor sandy roads, so that travel was difficult except on foot or on horseback or on the river. In many ways the people still observed ancestral habits that had long since dropped away as useless for Americans living in cities.

Thus Marjorie entered upon one of the great moments in her

life, partly in a spirit of sheer pixie-like relish for the adventure it promised, but mainly as a serious collector of the past. With her temperamental attraction to the old ways she found the same delight in collecting folkways, speech mannerisms, and hunting lore as other persons find in collecting antique furniture or dishes. She had to be selective, but she was quite disposed to ignore the new and seek out the old wherever she could find it, or ask questions of Miz' Piety Fiddia when the old ways no longer existed except in the memories of the older people. She stayed for two and a half months and brought back a full record. Her first spontaneous report was a long letter to Perkins written shortly after her return to Cross Creek: "I came back recently from very absorbing weeks lived with the old woman and her 'shiner son. . . . Well as I thought I knew the people of this particular section [I have] an entirely new conception of them. I knew they were gentle, honest. I knew that living was precarious, but just how hand-to-mouth it is, surprised me. I was also astonished by the *utter lack of bleakness or despair* in a group living momentarily on the very edge of starvation and danger. . . . I found a zestfulness in living, a humor, an alertness to beauty, quite unexpected, and of definite value to record. . . .

"These people are 'lawless' by an anomaly. They are living an entirely natural, and very hard, life, disturbing no one. Civilization has no concern with them, except to buy their excellent corn liquor and to hunt, in season, across their territory with an alarming abandon. Yet almost everything they do is illegal. And everything they do is necessary to sustain life in that place. The old clearings have been farmed out and will not 'make' good crops any more. The big timber is gone. The trapping is poor. They 'shine because 'shining is the only business they know that can be carried on in the country they know, and would be unwilling to leave. The 'shining will have to be the main thread of my story. But I want to make it dramatic by an entire absence of melodrama. It is quite simply a part of the background; a part of the whole resistance of the scrub country to the civilizing process. The scrub, as a matter of fact, has defeated civilization. It is one of the few areas where settlements have disappeared and the scanty population is constantly thinning. Just this side of the Oklawaha River, in the open range cattle country, the old-timers have recently heard their doom pronounced. The cattle must be fenced, which means the end of the old regime. A grand row has been raging there the past year, a Yankee family being whipped by the cattlemen for not minding their own business, and I shall use the situation. Several of the old cattlemen are 'kin' to the 'shiner families just across the river. . . .

"Possibly you wonder how I gain the confidence of these people without being a cold-blooded spy who intends to 'use' them. It is so easy for me to live their life with them, that I am in danger of losing all sophistication and perspective. I feel hurried sometimes, as though I must get 'written out' in this country within the next few years because so much is no longer strange or unusual to me. The life in the scrub is peculiarly right. While I was there I did all the illegal things too; stalked deer with a light at night, out of season, kept the family in squirrels, paddled the boat while my friend dynamited mullet, shot limpkin on the river edge and had to wade waist deep in cypress swamp to get him (and if you haven't eaten roast limpkin, you just haven't eaten, but you can go to county, state and federal jails for shooting them). But with food scarce these people kill quite correctly, I think, what they need. Incidentally, only what they need for food. The hunters with their licenses, on the other hand, kill a greater quantity during the legal season, and much of it is absolutely wasted—all of it entirely unneeded" [MKR to MEP November 4, 1931].

What her letter describes is a people living precariously on the fringe of a wilderness area which had felt the ravages of civilization but had successfully preserved itself against them. Her account reminds one of eighteenth-century theorists like Rousseau or Chateaubriand, who claimed that virtue would most abound in men who lived in a state of nature. These crackers living in the scrub seemed actually to *be* such people. They lived "an entirely natural life," if a very hard one. They were law-breakers, but only for forgivable reasons—because they must live, because they loved their wild country so deeply they would be unwilling to leave it and would do whatever they must to remain in it; because their law-breaking was part of a resistance to civilization. She undoubtedly meant it when she said that she could live their life easily, including the breaking of the law, because the life in the scrub was so peculiarly right, but her own participation has the air of a little girl playing at a fascinating game. This was a game she could play seriously, but as much as she admired the crackers and their ways, it was not a game she had to play for keeps, and they did. The thing she had to do was to return to her own, somewhat different, compromise with civilization at Cross Creek and write about what she had found in the Big Scrub.

She worked backward through time in her stories about the scrub. *South Moon Under* is chiefly about contemporary times, while *The Yearling* reflects a time fifty or sixty years earlier, before the partial despoiling of the wilderness. She was always scrupulous about historical accuracy, as about other details of the cracker way of life, and never confused horse-drawn times with later motor-driven times. Penny Baxter uses an old, untrustworthy, muzzle-loading rifle in the early part of *The Yearling;* Lant in *South Moon Under* uses a modern, high-powered rifle which he has bought through the Sears catalog. Still her treatment of cracker life in the scrub seems all of a piece because of a timelessness inherent in the material itself, because she depicts mainly those aspects of life which were the most traditional or the least affected by time. There is little difference in kind between Lant and Cleve trailing a wildcat through the scrub in the 1920's and Penny and Jody Baxter trailing a bear through the scrub in the 1870's. Most of the events she chooses to record are part of a way of life which was itself isolated from the stream of history in the great world, so that while most of the action in *South Moon Under* takes place in the Roaring Twenties, almost nothing of that roar penetrates the silence of the scrub. One is so thoroughly immersed in the scrub point of view that the local dispute involving the fencing of cattle is of larger importance than the Wall Street Crash. Historical time can be established definitely in *The Yearling* only by two unobtrusive references to Penny's having served in the Confederate army during the Civil War. The effect of this timelessness in her books about the scrub is to produce a detachment which heightens immediacy and makes more convincing the characters and events within the books.

Taken together her stories of the Florida cracker depict an entire way of life from childhood through courtship and marriage and the pains and joys of mature life to old age and death. Cracker social life is seen from many sides. "Jacob's Ladder" opens with a square dance, *South Moon Under* with a fence-raising, *Golden Apples* with a funeral. The stories contain a compendium of the cracker ways of making a living, with detailed accounts of everything from the planting and harvesting of corn and sweet potatoes to the more picturesque activities of trapping otter, 'gatoring, illegal seining on Lake Lochloosa, snake-hunting, and the cutting and rafting of cypress on the Oklawaha. From these stories one could learn how to fish for bream on Orange Lake or for bass on Hopkins Prairie in the scrub; how to find a bee-tree and get a washtub of honey from it; how to fire-hunt deer at night; how to build and operate a moonshine still, including how to hide the whiskey from the law and get it to the customers in Jacksonville.

Her books contain an extensive backwoods pharmacopeia, so that from them one could learn how to cure "risin's" with a soap and honey poultice or a prickly-pear pad; how to cure chills and fever by tying nine knots in a string dipped in turpentine and wearing it around the waist for nine days. She gives an unusually rich record of folklore: a hat turned inside out will quiet a bothersome screech owl; onion skins burned in the kitchen stove will keep quarreling out of the house; a dead alligator dragged under a house will drive away fleas. Because the crackers lived initimately with the world of nature, her books contain an elaborate lore of nature, some of it going back to ancient times. She shows how these people consulted the Zodiac for the proper sign in which to plant crops, or to geld hogs, or to cure meat; how they could predict the severity of the coming winter by studying the hair on mules or the hairy caterpillars; how they governed their hunting and fishing by close reference to the phase of the moon. The title of her first novel is a folk phrase reflecting the cracker sensitivity to the movements of the heavenly bodies. Walking through the scrub at night Lant considers the effect of the moon on the wild creatures: "The deer and the rabbits, the fish and the owls, stirred at moon-rise and at moon-down; at south-moon-over and at south-moon-under. The moon swung around the earth, or the earth swung around the moon, he was not sure. The moon rose in the east and that was moon-rise. Six hours later it hung at its zenith between east and west, and that was south-moon-over. It set in the west and that was moon-down. Then it passed from sight and swung under the earth, between east and west. And when it was directly under the earth, that was south-moon-under" [*SMU*, 109].

Unobtrusively, but continuously, the smallest, homeliest details of daily life are given—Ma Baxter scouring the floor with a corn-shucks scrub, Penny Baxter melting lead at the fire for his bullet mold, the women in *South Moon Under* "piecin'" quilts in the evening after dinner, the mode of cooking the staple foods from pork backbone and "purloo" to sweet potato pie. Such details are particularly rich in *The Yearling* where Marjorie indulged her nostalgic love of the old ways by giving elaborate little set pieces like the description of the interior of the old country store at Fort Volusia: "Jody walked along the length of the glass case under the counter. There were sweet crackers and an assortment of candies. There were Barlow knives and the new Rogers. There were shoe-strings, buttons, thread and needles. The coarser wares were on shelves that lined the walls. Buckets and pitchers, lard-oil lamps and basins, the new kerosene lamps, coffee pots and cast-iron skillets and Dutch ovens, nestled together like strange birds, fledglings in one nest. Beyond the utensils were the dress goods; calico and Osnaburg, denim and shoddy, domestic and homespun. A few bolts of alpaca and linsey and broadcloth were thick with dust.

There was little sale for such luxuries, especially in the summer. At the back of the store were the groceries, hams and cheeses and bacons. There were barrels of sugar and flour and meal and grits and green coffee beans; sacks of potatoes; kegs of syrup; barrels of whiskey. Nothing here was tempting and Jody wandered back to the glass case" [*Y*, 110].

From the day of her arrival in Florida she was attracted to the cracker dialect, and her early notes are full of jotted phrases which show her trying to catch its special cadence and idiom. A manuscript dating from the summer of 1930 records her attempt to analyze its distinctive features: "Cracker speech is a certain sign of the isolation of the Florida interior. It is astonishingly grammatical to one accustomed to mid-west and eastern rural slaughter of syntax. It is grammatical as old English is, with a definitely Chaucerian cast. I believe it to be similar to the speech of the Georgia and Carolina mountains. It differs from ordinary good English in its special idioms, its localized use of certain words, and in its Chaucerian plurals. It is well-enunciated and precise, without the drawl of Virginia and Maryland. . . . 'Posts' are 'postes,' 'ants' are 'antses.' The 'red-bird' is the 'reddy-bird.' The 'frog' is the 'toady-frog.' There is a tendency to slip an extra 'a' in wherever possible, so that a cracker child sees a 'wasap's nest in a palametto.' A prairie is a 'pararie.' . . . Ripples on the water are 'riffles.' There is a purely local use of the word 'belong.' 'Blueberries belong to be in this field.' 'The new preacher belongs to have a better circuit.' "

Marjorie never had formal training in linguistics, so that some of her attempts at analysis of the language were naïve. She recognized, for example, that many cracker locutions were archaic, but she described them indiscriminately as "Chaucerian" at one time and "Elizabethan" at another. She thought also that the relative lack of "drawl" in cracker speech was due to the fact that the crackers had never had Negro servants and therefore had never had their speech "corrupted" from this source.

But whatever the lack in her linguistic sophistication, there was no lack in the sharpness of her ear and in the astonishing retentiveness of her memory. After she finished the first draft of *South Moon Under* she took the manuscript back over to the scrub and asked Leonard Fiddia to read it for accuracy of fact and language. He was amazed at the fullness of detail and the uncanny accuracy. "Morge," he said, "either you got the best damn memory or else you done a hell of a lot of writing when you was over here" [Quoted in McGuire, 47]. Both things were true. Marjorie had stayed up late each night under her mosquito netting scribbling furiously on yellow foolscap to record the day's events and every scrap of dialect she thought she might use, but there is no doubt that she also had "the best damn memory" for cracker talk. By the middle thirties she had so well stocked her mind with the dialect that she could write "cracker" from memory with little recourse to either notes or to native speakers.

In most of her stories Marjorie uses cracker speech only in actual dialogue, the major portion of the narrative being given in standard English. In the early writings, like "Cracker Chidlings," she is obviously self-conscious about the dialect, still straining for accuracy, and she makes extensive use of misspellings and sprinkles apostrophes liberally across the page to show omitted sounds. Her transcription is accurate enough phonetically, but the "fly-speck" technique creates an impediment for the reader, as in this passage from "A Crop of Beans": "Ain't you sick o' keepin' Drenna hangin' around where you kin look at her all the day? I ain't done laughin', the way you begun a-courtin' her, like you was huntin' a squirrel goin' acrost a oak thicket an' you tryin' to keep sight of it" [*WTW*, 2].

In the later stories, she learned to make the dialect less obtrusive and used a more suggestive technique, letting idiom and syntax and grammar rather than distortions of spelling convey the flavor of the speech. Penny Baxter in the following passage is describing the first encounter with Ol' Slewfoot:

"Well," Penny began, "he takened us plumb by surprise."
Jody shivered.
"He slipped in like a shadow and killed our brood-sow. Laid her open, end to end, and only ate a mouthful. Not hongry. Jest low-down and mean."

Penny paused to light his own pipe. The Forresters bent to him with blazing splinters of fat pine.

"He come as quiet as a black cloud, into the wind. Made a circle to git his wind right. So quiet, the dogs never heered nor scented him. Even this un—even this un—" he leaned to stroke the feice at his feet—"was fooled" [*Y*, 59].

In *The Yearling* the dialect is handled so skillfully that one is seldom conscious of it, except for the occasional use of some archaic turn of phrase which has now passed entirely from the standard speech. In one scene Jody is hoeing sweet potatoes in the hot sun and his father walks up behind him:

"A heap o' taters ain't it, son?"

"Hit's a mort of 'em" [*Y*, 196].

Marjorie's great gift for the vernacular is best seen in her comic stories, which are in the tradition of the frontier tall tale. They have the classic elements established by Mark Twain—a folk narrator speaking in the vernacular, a surface realism coupled with wild exaggeration. The characters are grotesques. Quincy Dover, who narrates three of the best of these stories, weighs nearly 300 pounds; Uncle Benny Mathers, the constable of Oak Bluff, looks like a mischievous, satanic billy goat. But with all their grotesquerie, the people in these stories are humanly believable. Much of the comic comes from an indulgence in straight farce—Quincy Dover sprawled out, all 300 pounds of her, on the limb of a camphor tree spying down on the cockfights she has forbidden her husband to attend, and no reader surprised or disappointed when the limb breaks and drops Quincy into the midst of a cockfight. But as in other stories in this genre, much of the delight comes from a sheer relish in the vernacular language itself. "Alligators" begins like this with the true cadence and swing of folk speech: "Bless Katy, I don't know nothing about alligators. You belong to talk to some of them real old timey Florida 'gator hunters that has messed up with 'em deliberate. I don't never mess up with no alligator. If so chance me and one meets, it's just because he comes up with me—I don't never try to come up with him. There ain't never been but once me and a alligator met more than accidental." With this typical disclaimer, the speaker then goes on to relate the most extravagant adventures with alligators.

Quincy Dover rolls words on her tongue with as much conscious savor as if she were eating a piece of her own syrup pie. In "Varmints" she describes a rum-drinking, tobacco-chewing mule which two of her neighbors have owned jointly and fought over for twenty-eight years. One of them named Luty has just given the mule a shaving from his plug of tobacco: " 'Luty,' I said, 'the creetur ain't natural.' The mule looked at me then. Iffen you'll notice, most animals don't look much at persons. But this mule looked at me and I knowed I was done looked at. Then he looked off again, chewing vigorous. He'd done forgot me, studying on whatever 'tis mules studies on. Then it come to me. He was knowing. That was it. He was knowing. He had a human kind of a look, blest if he didn't. And it was Luty hisself he looked like. He looked like Luty more'n most persons could of done. Pot-bellied and low-coupled and big-eyed and easy-going, and biggety, too. And chewing his tobaccy and looking at you sideways. I'll swear" [*WTW*, 137].

In another story Quincy describes Uncle Benny's old Ford like this: "In the seven years he'd had it, he'd all but drove it to pieces, and it looked like a rusty, mangy razor-back hog. The hood was thin and narrow, like a shoat's nose—you remember the way all Model-T Fords were built. It had no top to it, nor no doors to the front seat, and the back seat rose up in a hump where the bird-dogs had squeezed the excelsior chitlin's out of it" [*WTW*, 24]. The stories are sprinkled with sentences like these, in which the words are a joy to the ear and an easement to the imagination: "She looked me up and down like a woman trying to make up her mind to step on a cockroach."—"Doc climbed out of the Ford trembling like a dish of custard."—"Jim ain't change none, neither. Shingle-butted and holler chested and a mouth like a sewed-up buttonhole and light blue eyes as mean as the book of Job."—"He puttened the skimmings into barrels to make buck. When the buck was foaming and spitting and powerful enough to make a man see damnation under him, he run it through a little homemade still."—"I looked at her. I takened my tongue and flicked it, like a man flicking a fishing rod. I takened it like a casting line and I laid it down right where I wanted it."

The pleasure in exaggeration, in giving the stretch to the tall tale, shows in this passage from "Alligators": "Directly we sees a row of blubbers. That was the 'gator breathing. The blubbers stop, and Endy lets him have the harpoon. Ka-whow! Just back of his hind legs. Endy knowed right where to feel for him.

"Then bless Katy, here we go across the lake. We played out all our rope. I starts up the engine. You know we couldn't catch up with him? That 'gator was going better'n twelve miles a hour. He had to be, to keep the harpoon rope taut with the engine going. I threw it in reverse. It didn't no more'n slow him down a little. That 'gator was just naturally carrying us off. Sometimes it looked like he didn't have no more'n three feet of tail in the water. The rest of him was scrambling along on top. I never heered such a fuss. It sounded like fifteen oxen a-wallering in the water" [*WTW*, 224].

These comic stories are a major literary accomplishment, good enough to be placed beside the best of Ring Lardner or Faulkner or the other American writers of this century who have followed Mark Twain's lead in using folk narration. The creative accomplishment is more impressive when one recalls that these stories are the product not of a "native" who grew up with the sound of cracker speech in her ear, but of a city woman who acquired that speech, having heard it for the first time when she was past thirty. She filled these stories with her own exuberance and enthusiasm for the Florida cracker way of life, her own delight in the wit, the beauty, and the vividness of the language. One regrets that she never carried out her plan of the middle thirties to write enough of them to fill a volume.

Readers will detect a classic American note to Marjorie's writings in other ways than her skilled use of vernacular speech. Her books express many parts of what might be called a frontier archetype. Baxter's Island in *The Yearling* is hauntingly familiar to Americans: The simple cabin in a forest clearing, a split-rail fence surrounding a few acres wrested from the wilderness and planted to corn and beans, a pig or two, a cow and an old horse in a small barn near the house, the simple fare from the fields supplemented by game from the forest, most artifacts made by hand, most operations around the place performed by hand or with primitive machinery, as one would expect in a pre-industrial way of life where there was little money and little commerce except by barter. The only thing one misses is the redskin with his tomahawk, and in this omission Marjorie was simply being historically scrupulous, since the Indians had all been driven out of central Florida by the time the scrub was pioneered in the 1870's.

The central male figure in her stories has the same nostalgic familiarity. Penny Baxter, Lantry Jacklin, Luke Brinley, Mart, are, in differing proportions, blends of Cooper's Natty Bumppo and Jefferson's ideal husbandman. The woodsman-frontiersman has been depicted in a number of ways in American literature, from the savage mountain man who is a kind of white Indian, to the squalid, malaria-ridden, poor white. Marjorie's fiction contains no developed figure of the white savage, except possibly for the Forresters in *The Yearling*, who bear only approximate resemblance. And in like fashion, there are no more than brief glimpses of the degenerate clay-eater, even though her stories abound in figures who are in the lowest reaches of poverty. In her books even the most desperate poverty carries with it no necessary moral decline. Her people often look Ol' Starvation in the face and know him to look meaner than Ol' Slewfoot, but the experience teaches them hardihood and self-reliance rather than turpitude. Her cracker country contains few Snopeses or Jeeter Lesters.

One other conception of the frontiersman which has been most pervasive in literature, so pervasive as to achieve the dimension of a myth, is Cooper's conception of Natty Bumppo in *The Leatherstocking Tales*. Natty has the Indian's virtues of physical courage, endurance, great strength, and the power of instinctive action, as well as the white man's "gifts" of pity, humility, deference to womanhood, and a strong sense of personal honor. Cooper leaves no doubt that the reason this man is a paragon of physical and moral virtues is because he has been able to live at an ideally simple level in the great forest, far from the corrupting influences of civilization.

Several figures in the Rawlings stories, chiefly Penny Baxter and Lantry Jacklin, remind one of Natty. They show the same prowess as hunters and woodsmen, the same readiness and ability to meet crisis. They have little book learning, but are wise in the ways of the forest; they have the same quiet humor, the sensitivity to beauty, and the gentleness of spirit, combined with physical daring and skill. Each of these characters is also given his own individuality—Penny is diminutive in size from having been worked too hard on meager rations as a boy, and he is a farmer as much as he is a hunter; Lant is lean and gangling and is a moonshiner as well as a gifted woodsman. Both remind one of R. W. B. Lewis' "hero in space," the man like Natty Bumppo or Huck Finn who lights out for the territory when the irritants of civilization become too great.

A number of critics have pointed out a fundamental ambivalence in *The Leatherstocking Tales* whereby Cooper shows an obvious fondness for Natty and for his free and virtuous life in a wilderness Eden, but also allows Natty to be sadly mistreated by civilization and eventually driven to flight, as if his heart was with Natty but his head on the side of civilization. Marjorie's fiction shows this same ambivalence. One of her short stories called "The Enemy" concerns an irascible, hard-bitten old cattleman named Milford, whose family for several generations has grazed cattle in Florida on the unrestricted free range. The state legislature passes laws which require that all cattle be restrained behind fences, and one day Milford finds that his cattle are shut off from water during a drought because a stranger named Dixon has moved in, bought some of the old free range, and fenced it in. Milford rounds up his old friends and wishes to open a way to water by force. His friends refuse. One of them says, "Times has changed. Florida ain't the wild free place 'twere in my daddy's time nor even my time. Folks is buyin' up land and buildin' houses on it and farmin' land that ain't had nothin' on it for a thousand years but polecats and 'coons and 'possums and wildcats. And they got just as good a right to do it as we got to be settin' here." In this story Marjorie stands squarely on the side of civilization and Progress, but in most of her other writings neither law nor Progress fares so well. In "Jacob's Ladder," the law is one of the chief adversaries against which the young cracker couple must struggle in their effort to survive. In *South Moon Under,* civilization is a force of destruction which rapes the great cypress from the banks of the Oklawaha with snarling machines. The law is the prohibition agent who would destroy Lant's chief means of livelihood, or it is the game warden who would imprison him for taking the deer he needs for food. The measure of Lant's heroism is often the ingenuity and persistence with which he resists the laws of civilization.

The law which Marjorie approves in this novel is the unwritten, vigilante law of Lant's Uncle Abner, who gathers a band of men in the night to administer a whipping to the Streeters who have offended the community by penning other men's stock. Her antipathy for the law of the courts represents one more facet of her primitivism and is undoubtedly related to her emotional sympathy for her cracker friends as well as her general impatience with the irritations of civilization.

Cooper's novel *The Pioneers* shows Natty Bumppo, now growing old, being punished in jail for "poaching" a deer, an offense against a law which has only recently come with the settlers into an area over which he had hunted in complete freedom for many years. Marjorie's hunter friend, old Cal Long, who was in many ways a real-life Natty Bumppo, had an almost identical collision with the law when the Ocala National Forest was formed and took in the land his father had homesteaded in the scrub. In *Cross Creek* she describes his reaction: "All his way of life in the last of his nearly eighty years irked him. This was especially because a Federal game refuge had been established in the scrub, taking in his clearing. He was no longer allowed . . . to kill deer on his own land. But I noticed that venison continued a staple meat on his table.

" 'The law says I cain't shoot a buck in my own potato patch!' he raged. 'The law says I cain't kill me a wild turkey scratchin' up my cowpeas. The law this, the law that! Why,' he snorted, 'I'm too old a man to begin obeyin' the law!' " [*CC*, 236]. Her own temperamental sympathy with the old man is unmistakable, but there was a deeper ambivalence in her attitude toward civilization which shows in her depiction of Penny Baxter in *The Yearling.*

She applauds Penny Baxter's flight from the town into the wild scrub, and she gives him in his role as hunter and woodsman many of the attributes of Natty Bumppo, those virtues which are the result of living close to nature, but she also makes Penny a knowing and hard working farmer, who successfully fights off the incursions of wild creatures and holds the wilderness at bay as the agent of civilization. Thus he falls squarely into the image of the idealized agrarian freeholder, which has been pervasive in American culture since the eighteenth century. Penny chiefly displays his hunting prowess when he pursues Ol' Slewfoot as an aroused farmer avenging the slaughter of his stock. As an independent, self-reliant yeoman farmer living in a great forest, he is representative of a frontier condition midway between the savagery of the mountain men and the corruptions of sophisticated society, that agrarian middle ground esteemed by Crèvecoeur and Jefferson as the ideal condition for human happiness. To this frontier, so intimately associated with the American dream, Marjorie obviously has strong attachments, both theoretical and emotional.

Her use of this middle ground in her stories identifies her with an important American pastoral tradition which has begun to be explored by scholars only in recent years. In a book entitled *Virgin Land*, Henry Nash Smith has shown that during much of the nineteenth century when the great West was being settled, the imagination of the American people was dominated by a dream of transforming the wild heartland of the continent into a beautiful and productive garden. This concept was, according to Smith, largely a poetic idea containing many aspects of the American dream. It consisted of a master symbol, the garden, which included other metaphors of fecundity and blissful labor in the earth, and of a second major symbol in the center of the garden, the idealized husbandman or frontier farmer. In a more recent book, *The Machine in the Garden*, Leo Marx has extended Smith's thesis, demonstrating the presence in American culture of a pastoral tradition deriving ultimately from Virgil. Marx shows that many American writers have used what he calls "the syntax of the middle landscape"—a symbolic setting or background for their stories which they locate somewhere between the corruption of effete civilization and the barbarism of the howling wilderness. A sonnet by Frost called "The Vantage Point" provides a good illustration of the phenomenon, its very title expressing one of the main functions of this landscape. The poet describes a hillside pasture—his vantage point—a part of the earth subdued to man's use but neither wild like the forest further up the mountain, nor civilized like the town further down. From this place among the junipers, the poet can look across the valley and observe from a mediating distance the white houses which are the abode of living men or the white stones which indicate the abode of the dead. If weary of contemplating the affairs of men, the poet has only to turn on his arm to be able to contemplate the earth and the whole realm of nature. There are many versions of this landscape in American literature, but its physical particulars, according to Marx, are less important than its power as a metaphor, its ability to express esthetic, moral, political, and even religious values. Among the major authors who have written American versions of the pastoral, utilizing this symbolic middle landscape, Marx discusses Jefferson, Thoreau, Twain, Hemingway, Frost, and Fitzgerald. Marjorie clearly belongs to this company.

Her symbolic landscape was, in general, north central Florida, and her idealized husbandman was, in general, the cracker, but she refined more explicit versions of both. In *South Moon Under* her stress is upon the unspoiled wilderness and the beauties of nature, and her central figure is a man of the forest. In *Golden Apples* her stress is upon the agrarian, and her central figure is actually two: Luke Brinley, the cracker, who is the American husbandman motivated by a familiar passion to convert the wild jungle hammock into a productive orange grove; and Tordell, the Englishman, who undergoes another of the archetypal experiences of the American pastoral. Driven forth unjustly from his European home into bitter exile, he undergoes a regeneration in the New World, becoming a new man by acquiring the American vision of fruitful toil in a garden which he will help to wrest from the jungle.

Marjorie truly loved the deep woods, but as much as she idealized their peace and beauty, she knew that few men could remain in them permanently except as the Baxters do in *The Yearling*—in an island, a garden cultivated in the midst of the forest, and in this book she brings together both ends of her pastoral vision to produce her image of the ideal place for human life. She explicitly insists upon the balance between the wild and the civilized. On one of his visits to Grandma Hutto at Fort Volusia, Jody wrestles with the question of whether he would prefer to stay with Grandma where he has fine food and the niceties of civilization, or return to the rougher life of the scrub. His answer comes as he pictures in his mind the cabin in the clearing: "Hoot-owls would be crying, and perhaps the wolves would howl, or a panther scream. The deer would be drinking at the sink-hole, the bucks alone, the does with their fawns. The bear cubs would be curled up in their beds together. There was something at Baxter's Island that was better than white tablecloths and counterpanes" [*Y*, 120-21]. That something was the wildness. On another occasion when Jody has been out hunting with the grown-ups following the great storm, he is so ecstatic with the shooting and the camping and the talk around the fire at night that he thinks he would like to stay out in the woods forever. But then on the return home when he first sees the familiar tall pines of Baxter's Island, he is flooded with a comfortable warmth of joy to be coming home, and he knows that one can have too much of the wild as he can have too much of the civilized. In this novel, Penny Baxter exemplifies the man who has learned to live in the happy middle ground between the two.

Marjorie's pastoralism was two-ply; she not only wrote about a symbolic garden of the middle landscape, she lived in one, and the charming account of that experience is *Cross Creek.* This book, which defies classification according to customary literary types, drops neatly into the slot labelled "pastoral idyll." It is one of the best examples of the genre in recent literature. In this book the quite ordinary people and events she writes about gain significance because of a luminous quality cast over them by her special way of viewing them. The mixture of humorous anecdote, serious meditation, character sketch, nature description, talk about food, superstition, the seasons of the year, is bound together by an attitude, the pastoral viewpoint, which is reflected in the opening pages of the book where she tries to explain why she was attracted to Cross Creek: "We at the Creek need and have found only very simple things. We must need flowering and fruiting trees, for all of us have citrus groves of one size or another. We must need a certain blandness of season, with a longer and more beneficent heat than many require. . . . We need the song of birds, and there is none finer than the redbird. We need the sound of the rain coming across the *hamaca*, and the sound of wind in trees—and there is no more sensitive Aeolian harp than the palm. . . .

"We need above all, I think, a certain remoteness from urban confusion, and while this can be found in other places, Cross Creek offers it with such beauty and grace that once entangled with it, no other place seems possible to us" [*CC*, 3].

The grove was literally, for more than a dozen years, her vantage point, from which she could look reflectively back toward the city or out toward the wilderness of the scrub. Her commitment to a pastoral viewpoint was quite knowing and self-conscious. Though she was not a learned person, she was widely read, and somewhere, probably in her French classes at the University of Wisconsin, she had run across George Sand's bucolic idyll, *La Mare au Diable* (*The Haunted Pool*). In notes written soon after her arrival in Florida she quotes the following passage from George Sand, a passage she later used in *Cross Creek:* "Nature possesses the secret of happiness, and no one has been able to steal it from her. The happiest of men would be he who, working intelligently and laboring with his hands, drawing comfort and liberty from the exercise of his intelligent strength, should have time to live through his heart and his brain, to comprehend his own work and that of God. Happiness would be wherever the mind, the heart and the arm should work together beneath the eye of Providence, so that a holy harmony should exist between the munificence of God and the rapture of the human soul." Then a little further on in her notes, Marjorie also copied another passage from George Sand which contained a quotation from Virgil, one of the fountainheads of the pastoral tradition: "And the dream of a sweet, free, poetic, laborious and simple life is not so difficult to conceive that it need be dismissed as a chimera. Virgil's sad but sweet words 'O, happy the man of the fields, if he but knew his happiness!' are a regret; but like all regrets they are also a prediction. A day will come when the husbandman will be able to be an artist also—if not to express—at least to feel the beautiful."

There is no doubt that she thought of herself at Cross Creek as a kind of Virgilian husbandman or shepherdess, and occasionally used phrases in her book such as "we tillers of the soil," which express her desire to be identified with her neighbors who actually were committed to rural or agricultural pursuits. She meant the grove to be her Walden Pond, where like Thoreau she could front the essential facts of life, or perhaps more accurately, her Brook Farm, the place where she would achieve that holy harmony of mind and muscle which would produce the highest kind of human happiness. She soon discovered, as Hawthorne did at Brook Farm, that the writing demanded precedence, and as soon as she was able to hire others, her own labors at the grove became either supervising or puttering, while she submitted more and more to the anguish of the typewriter. But during the first three or four years at the Creek she grubbed enough in the earth to learn what it was actually like to be a husbandman and to feel entitled to call herself a tiller of the soil.

She undoubtedly hoped that she would be one of those husbandmen who would be the artist also, able to express the beautiful which she knew she felt in a deep and compelling way. Beauty was of prime importance in her whole outlook, one of those centers from which lines radiate out to touch most of her other ideas and attitudes. Her esthetic, which also embraced an ethic, began not surprisingly, in her doctrine of adjustment to an environment, and might be summarized as follows: There is no single absolute Beauty, but only a beauty relative to every man's particular experience of life. One cannot see the beauty around him, cannot therefore have joy of his life, unless he is spiritually in harmony with his setting; one cannot be in harmony with his setting if he is full of greed, despair, bitterness, or cowardice. Her notes for the lecture, "The Invisible Florida," contain an illustrative anecdote: "Two people can stand side by side and look at a Florida hammock. One sees only an obnoxious tangle and imagines rattlesnakes under every palmetto. The other sees beauty. I was duck hunting with two men one morning on Orange Lake. We crossed the lake just at dawn. The moon was setting and the sun was rising. It was a world of saffron and silver. One man said, 'Isn't it beautiful?' and the other said, 'What's beautiful? Where are the ducks?' " She was deeply convinced that one of the general ills of modern life, particularly for people in cities, was this preoccupation with "the ducks," with utilitarian busyness of one kind or another, so that they were unable to see the beauty with which they were surrounded, even in cities.

It was one of the main intentions of her art, as of much other pastoral art, not only to present scenes of quiet beauty, but to evoke a new awareness of the relation between beauty and virtue. *Golden Apples* is almost tractarian in its insistence on this theme. Tordell has to purge himself of cowardice and bitterness and a sense of defeat before he can see the beauty of the Florida hammockland, but when he does he undergoes a dramatic regeneration and is able to join himself in spiritual oneness with the earth he works and thus participate in the beauty and strength of the very cosmos. It was the unconscious courage of the crackers in the scrub which made them seem beautiful to

Marjorie and which accounted for the serenity in their lives, though they lived with hunger and danger. This courage becomes the central ethic of *The Yearling*, a stoic acceptance of the kind which ennobles the character of Penny Baxter, a truth which Jody learns with pain, but which makes him a man. It is the hard wisdom which Penny conveys to his son in these words: "You figgered I went back on you. . . . Boy, life goes back on you. . . . Ever' man wants life to be a fine thing, and a easy. 'Tis fine, boy, powerful fine, but 'tain't easy. Life knocks a man down and he gits up and it knocks him down agin. I've been uneasy all my life. . . . What's he to do when he gits knocked down? Why, take it for his share and go on" [*Y*, 426].

Marjorie's commitment to the pastoral was strong enough to survive her leaving Cross Creek and even her leaving Florida itself, and her last book, *The Sojourner*, takes the form of a pastoral allegory. Her sojourner, Ase Linden, is the clearest example in her books of the idealized husbandman, keeping his fertile garden in the symbolic middle landscape, located now in southern Michigan rather than Florida. He is balanced between the primitive, which comes to him from his spiritual father, Mink, the last of the Fisher Indians, and the acquisitive greed of the white man's civilization which is all around him in his mother, his wife, and above all in his children. His children give themselves to the crassest kind of materialism and eventually become his literal enemies, who seek to take his farm by legal trickery and turn it into a cheap housing development for factory workers. To save his farm, Ase conveys it in a will to his spiritual son, Jan Rabaski, the child of Polish immigrants, who will continue to work it as a productive garden after his death.

Aside from her pantheism and her transcendental nature doctrines, the most pervasive theme in Marjorie's writings is a mystique of the earth resembling that found in Steinbeck and Faulkner, a quasi-religious doctrine which motivated her own life at Cross Creek and which she found confirmed and illustrated in the lives of the crackers she had known on the Florida frontier: The secret of human happiness is to commit oneself in love to that portion of the earth with which one can feel a bond of harmony, and this will flood life with joy and give strength to withstand whatever adversities life might bring. Preferably this means that one should labor in the earth in humble obedience to its laws, as Marjorie shows all her idealized husbandmen doing, creating beauty and fruitfulness in that garden of the pastoral middle ground, grafting the sweet orange twigs onto the sour root stock of the wild hammock oranges to make a symmetrical grove where only jungle stood before. Such harmony with the earth, like the communion one can achieve with wild nature, will fill life with beauty and joy because it brings union ultimately with the cosmos itself. The doctrine is given explicitly at the end of *Golden Apples* where she is describing the Englishman's "transfiguration": "Tordell spraddled his legs in the sand. As he stood, a great content possessed him. It seemed to him that the inviolable pulse of earth beat upward through his veins like sap. Nothing could strike him while he stood so joined to it.

"A man was a puny thing, frightened and lonely; transitory and unimportant. When he blended himself with whatever was greater than he, he found peace. He shared the importance of growth and continuity. When a man shaped growth to his ends, he put his hand on the secret core of creation, and in the shaping was a moment's mastery, and in the mastery was his dignity. He joined himself to the earth, and because the earth itself was a little part of a farther universe, he joined himself through it to the stars, and in the union was his ecstasy" [*GA*, 351].

Her own earth-feeling was so strong that she not only insisted a man should join himself with earth, she also turned this around and tended to see human character as a projection of landscape. All her discussion of the crackers makes the assumption that they are the kind of people they are because of *where* they are. A letter dating from the fall of 1935 gives an explicit example of this habit of mind. Immediately after sending the final draft of *Golden Apples* off to Scribner's in August, Marjorie climbed onto a train with a sigh of relief and went to visit her brother Arthur in Seattle. He took her on an exciting boat trip to Alaska up the inland waterway. Back in Florida in November, she wrote to Perkins: "I hate to tell you, Max, but I'm afraid that sometime in the next three or four years I shall have to go to Alaska to spend a year or so and write a novel. A whole set of characters, a motif, suggested themselves to me, irresistibly requiring that setting and no other. I had to fight staying there to do it right then. You see, with the acute feeling I have for the relation of man to his natural background, that dark and forbidding mountainous country offers a setting for the theme of betrayal. Human treachery is the most appalling thing. You have to learn to expect to be betrayed. Yet you must never learn to betray. So I give you fair warning, if things get too thick for me here or too unhappy, I shall have to clear out for that part of the world. The story is already a unit" [MKR to MEP November 5, 1935].

For a similar reason she chose a northern setting for her last novel and felt it necessary to go herself to the midst of that setting in order to finish the book. "Ase Linden, the sojourner, might have lived anywhere," she wrote, "but since a specific nature background is always necessary for me, I could only see him in a sterner land than the Florida of which I have previously written. He moved against snow and ice, and the sharp changes of the northern seasons were part of his blood and bones" [MS, UF Library].

Her own earth-feeling was so ecstatic and mystic at times that she was led to make a renunciation of the sort made by Faulkner's Ike McCaslin in *Go Down, Moses*. Ike refused to accept inheritance of the McCaslin plantation which was to come to him, because he became convinced that the earth cannot be owned but only used under God's suzerainty, that the curse which lies upon it comes from the white man's greed for ownership. This is the reason why the last of Marjorie's ideal husbandmen, the sojourner Ase Linden, is never moved to acquire title to the land he works for nearly eighty years. What seems an almost perverse indifference to ownership on his part is understandable only in terms of his conviction that nothing tangible *belongs* to any man. This was Marjorie's own conviction. In the final chapter of *Cross Creek* she makes a statement which reminds one of the Physiocrats in eighteenth-century France: "It seems to me that the earth may be borrowed but not bought. It may be used, but not owned. It gives itself in response to love and tending, offers its seasonal flowering and fruiting. But we are tenants not possessors, lovers and not masters" [*CC*, 368].

In this spirit, she consigns her Cross Creek property to the redbirds, to the wind and the rain, to the cosmic secrecy of seed.

A column of smoke rose from the cabin

. The smoke was blue where it left the red of the clay ... trailed into the blue of the sky and was no longer blue but gray.
The boy Jody watched it, speculating. The fire on the kitchen hearth was dying away. His mother was hanging up the pots and pans after the noon dinner. The day was Friday. She would sweep the floor with a broom of ti-ti and then, if he were lucky, she would scrub it with the corn-shucks scrub ... miss him until he had reached the creek. He stood a minute, balancing the hoe on his shoulder.

The clearing itself was pleasant if the unweeded rows of young shafts of corn were not before him. The wild bees had found the chinaberry tree by the front gate. They burrowed into the fragile lavender blooms as

6

The Literary Artist

Ellen Glasgow, in her autobiographical book, *A Certain Measure*, looking back over a long writing career which had included a number of distinguished regionalist novels based on her native Virginia, made this comment about regionalist fiction: "The creative writer soon learns that when the central character has come to life, when the blood quickens in his veins . . . his immediate surroundings will awaken and respond to this sudden glow of animation. . . . The power to create life is the staple of fiction. When the novelist possesses this one thing needful, all else, or very nearly all else may be acquired" [163-64].

Miss Glasgow's insistence that character and not place should come first in regionalist fiction as in any other kind of fiction, highlights Marjorie Kinnan Rawlings' basic problem as a literary artist, since in most of her major writings *place* undoubtedly came first. When she began to write about Florida, her principal motive was to record rather than to create, and for a long time fiction was for her chiefly a vehicle by which to express fact. In the early years of their dialogue-by-mail, Perkins' suggestions for revision nearly always urged Marjorie to greater emphasis on the fictive elements of character and story and less on the reporting of fact. She was always willing to move in this direction, but she confessed openly by way of apology for the prosiness of the first draft of "Jacob's Ladder," "You see, I began with my mind full of this environment" [MKR to MEP n.d. (Spring, 1931)]. In response to his suggestion that she give more emphasis to story in *South Moon Under* she wrote, "Reading over the manuscript of *South Moon Under*, I am astonished at how far I went out of my way to be random and rambling. The direct narrative form throughout is so patently required—and through so much of the book I seem perversely to have avoided it. Looking back at my earliest conception of the book, I do not believe that I ever planned it as a true novel, but as you express it, as a 'social chronicle' " [MKR to MEP August 31, 1932].

During her entire career Marjorie was caught in the regionalist's typical dilemma of how to strike the proper balance between fact and fiction, and she left an extensive record of her attempts to deal with the problem theoretically. Speaking to a creative writing class at the University of Florida in 1938, she said, "We can safely say that fact is the background of literature. But facts themselves are not an open sesame to good writing. It is a common error to believe that travel, adventure, contact with many people and many kinds of people will automatically provide the writer with material. Whether they provide material or not depends on the writer's ability to absorb them into himself. . . . Facts are unreliable and treacherous. Or perhaps I should say that a writer's judgment of their artistic value is unreliable and treacherous. Facts let you down. . . . Strangely enough facts used literally in fiction often do not carry a conviction of truth. . . . The two most factual pieces of fiction I have ever written were rejected because the editors said they were not plausible. [She is probably referring to "Lord Bill of the Suwannee River," and to an unpublished story based on her friend Dessie Smith entitled "Donnie Get Your Gun."] Facts alone are empty, meaningless, valueless, inartistic and dangerous. What then happens to facts to turn them into fiction? The writer happens to them. The writer must give them credulity. He must give them meaning. He must give them artistic unity. Above all, he must give them the breath of life. . . . I see a fact as an empty cup, to be filled with the prismatic fluid of the creative imagination. . . . The sense of reality is only the imaginative awareness of actuality." Her theoretical position is similar to that of Wallace Stevens, who insisted as strenuously as any poet in modern times on the radical importance of the creative imagination in imposing order on an otherwise formless, chaotic universe.

There would not seem to be much disparity between Marjorie's insistence that the writer must give "fact" the breath of life through the power of his creative imagination, and Ellen Glasgow's insistence that the staple of fiction is the power to create life. Actually there is a great difference. Miss Glasgow conceives of an imaginatively created human being, a fictive character undergoing a fictive life, placed in a setting which his vitality then imbues with life. Marjorie conceives of a much more diffuse external reality—"the facts"—which the radiant power of the artist's imagination imbues with life, so that in effect the external reality is *created* by the artist. Life is conceived by Ellen Glasgow in the first instance as *human* life and personality; by Marjorie it is conceived of as a setting or landscape which may or may not contain a human personality as one of its parts.

It is possible to come still closer to her concept of the artist's creative function by looking at a remark she made in a note intended as a preface to the story "Alligators," in *When the Whippoorwill.* In this note she explained how she had acquired much of the substance of the story from Fred Tompkins, and that she promised him half the proceeds if she sold the story. Some months later she received an unexpectedly large sum for the piece and went around to pay Fred his half. He was away and his wife refused to take the several hundred dollars Marjorie offered, saying that it was too much. Marjorie insisted, reminding her that much of the material in the story had come from Fred. "I know, honey," Mrs. Tompkins answered, "but tellin' is one thing and composin' is another." This, said Marjorie, was a distinction she recommended to all realists and regional writers who mistake fact for art.

The note was never used because Marjorie decided it would inject an undesirable journalistic touch into the book. She decided in this case to emphasize "composin'," the kind of running decision she was forced to make during her entire career. In "composin' " the writer gives order to the raw data of experience and adds the heat of imagination which fuses them into the new substance of art. This is exactly what happened in "Alligators." Marjorie may have started with a sheaf of notes containing a number of Fred Tompkins' alligator yarns, and with her head full of the sound of his cracker speech, but she then created a narrator, a fictive person whose voice tells the story. This was not Fred Tompkins, though the accents may have been his. It was an imagined person, behind whose voice was an ordering intelligence which converted the raw material of her notes into a single, new thing which had a resonance and life of its own.

But Marjorie's preoccupation with "tellin'," with sending back a full report of what it was like in her frontier Eden, explains the structural looseness of the early writings. In "Cracker Chidlings" the order of the sketches could be shuffled or they could be added to or diminished in number with little change in total effect. "Jacob's Ladder" moves several steps toward literature by concentrating upon a single cracker couple and their struggle to survive, but the narration still is loose and rambling, a picaresque progression from one hardship to another, and the story's chief value lies in its vivid portrayal of cracker life seen against magnificent panels of Florida scenery. The cracker couple, Mart and Florrie, are closely reproduced from life, and perhaps for that reason never quite come to life. They were a couple who lived in the tenant house at the grove for a time after Marjorie first came to the Creek, though they soon moved on because the proud young man found grove work not to his taste. Marjorie tells in *Cross Creek* how the small, tawny, soft-spoken woman haunted her so that she wrote of her again as Allie in *Golden Apples.* The account of the young couple's adventures in "Jacob's Ladder" is clearly not far removed from a record of Marjorie's personal observations of cracker life.

After Perkins' urging, she went back over her first draft of *South Moon Under* and tried to give the book "true novel form" by telling the story of how a typical family came to settle in the scrub. She represented the man Lantry, in flight from the law, having killed a revenue officer in Virginia and fleeing to central Florida, then marrying a local woman and moving across the Oklawaha River into the wild scrub as a further sanctuary from pursuit. Lantry's children grow up there and marry, including Piety, who marries Willy Jacklin from the flat-woods side of the Oklawaha. Their son Lant is born in the scrub, brought up completely indigenous to the wilderness, and the major part of the book tells of his struggle for existence in the wild country he loves. Lant and his mother Piety were closely modeled upon Leonard Fiddia and his mother Piety, and most of the major incidents in the book, including the treachery of the cousin in betraying Lant to the revenuers, were transcribed closely from life. Since Marjorie was chiefly interested in setting forth an unusual region and way of life, the people in this book all seem instrumental to that purpose. They are much more typical crackers than they are unique human beings. This remains a book of unusual beauty and significance and a worthy literary achievement because the cracker way of life is given with color and vibrancy and the wilderness background with a fresh lyric beauty.

Her difficulties with *Golden Apples* we have already sufficiently described. It is ironic that in this book where unity is so conspicuously lacking she was trying to write a story having a tight, well-made plot. Her handling of character in this work gives further insight into the nature of her creative talent. When she ran into trouble bringing the Englishman Tordell to life, it is revealing that her instinctive reaction was not to fall back on a more intensive creative effort but to seek out an actual Englishman whom she could interview. She discovered such a man, now advanced in years, who had come to Florida with two brothers in the 1880's and had planted a citrus grove only to see it destroyed in the freeze of 1895. She went up to Jacksonville, where the man was working as an agent of the Clyde steamship line, to ask him, as she wrote Perkins, "innumerable 'lead' questions, whose answers should keep me on the right track" [MKR to MEP November 4, 1931]. When this did not prove enough, she made the voyage two years later to England to have firsthand experience of the Hampshire setting from which she intended her Englishman to come, and then to write a version of the story whose opening scenes were laid in England, only to feel obliged later to throw all this away. With all these essentially journalistic efforts, she never succeeded in making Tordell a convincing human being.

Her difficulty with this book was not due to a lack of worthy intention or a lack of hard work. During the whole long process of writing she kept begging Perkins for his sternest criticism. "Don't ever be polite about my stuff, the truth is the greatest kindness" [MKR to MEP August 9, 1934]. "Don't spare me. You know I don't mind work and it is hard to hurt my feelings. Anything to get it right" [MKR to MEP July 31, 1934]. Disgusted with the book's failure, she told him after she got over some of the chagrin: "I don't blame anyone but myself for *Golden Apples* being interesting trash instead of literature. But you should have bullied and shamed me further. I can do better than that and you know it" [MKR to MEP October 15, 1935]. She blamed her failure on her "old difficulty with actual truth," meaning that she had been too preoccupied with actual historical events like the Big Freeze of 1895 and with characters too closely modeled on life.

The Yearling was the first of her major works where she found the ideal point of balance between fact and fiction. She had already put the scrub on record in *South Moon Under*, so she was untroubled by this compulsion and free to make more purely literary use of the same materials. She chose a time far enough back in the past to appeal strongly to her antiquarian tastes and to provide exactly the right esthetic distance to force her imagination rather than her reporter's sense into full play. Most important of all, she started for the first time with a primary concern for character rather than place, with the boy Jody as a single dominant character, and she gave the story a stiff backbone of theme, one of the oldest and most universal in literature, the painful passage of a boy from childhood into manhood.

She gave other aspects of the book a classic discipline. She placed point of view with Jody, and though she had a struggle after the story began to develop to keep Penny Baxter from taking it over, she persisted, and the narrative stayed with Jody. Time was strictly controlled to a single year's passage from April to April. The main characters were limited in number to the three members of the Baxter family—actually to Jody and the two beings he loved most, his father and his pet fawn. Ma Baxter, less fully realized, is a kind of scolding negative presence, full of duty and frugality and a puritanical distaste for pleasure. All other characters were held to minor supporting function and never allowed to obtrude upon the central grouping. Place was confined to the scrub, and chiefly to Baxter's Island within the scrub, except for brief excursions to Fort Volusia which lay just outside the scrub's boundaries. The important symbol of the flutter mill with which the book opens and closes gives an envelope structure to the action. The continuous parallel symbolism of the fawn reinforces the yearling status of Jody and makes more poignant his passage into manhood.

Marjorie's narrative talent was chiefly that of a raconteur, a teller of tales, and she always shows best in the short haul in particular scenes and anecdotes. Because of its controlling theme, there is a sense of steady progression in *The Yearling*, of a large inclusive action—Jody passes from boyhood to manhood, and his father from vigorous maturity to the beginning of broken old age. But within this structural pattern, because point of view resides with Jody, she is able to make the book a sequence of revelations and reflections, an indefinite series of carefully realized individual scenes, as if a spotlight were swung from one facet of life in the scrub to another. Jody is "addled" by the beauty of an April day; he goes on a bear hunt with his father; he visits the Forresters while his father swaps a worthless dog for a good shotgun; he rides out with the men on a two-day exploration of the scrub after the great rain; he frolics along a forest path with his fawn; he goes through the agony of the fawn's death and the three-day descent into the valley of hunger and separation from his father. Anecdotes are told by the dozen, most often by Penny.

One reason for *The Yearling*'s excellence as fiction is that in this book the characters were conceived of as people first and as crackers second. All the main characters are almost entirely fictional, though many of their particular traits and many of the incidents in their lives were suggested from real life. Penny Baxter bears little resemblance to Reuben Long, his real-life counterpart who first homesteaded Pat's Island in the scrub, and Jody Baxter has no specific resemblance to either of Reuben's sons, Mel or Cal, from whom Marjorie had much information about early life in the scrub. The Forresters in the novel were based upon a family of Sullivans who lived (as depicted in the book) about four miles west of Pat's Island at a place which is now called Hughes Island. The Sullivans, like the Forresters, farmed very little, but lived from their cattle, from hunting, fishing, and horsetrading, and from moonshining. Grandma Hutto and her sailor son Oliver had no real-life counterparts and came close to being the kind of romantic cliché which often resulted from Marjorie's attempts to create character wholly from imagination.

At times Marjorie was quite aware of her own limitations as a creator of character, and once wrote in a letter to Fitzgerald, "You have what must actually be a painful insight into people, especially complicated people. I don't understand people like us —and what little I do understand, terrifies me. That's why I write, gratefully, of the very simple people whose problems are only the most fundamental and primitive ones. I have probably been more cowardly than I'd admit, in sinking my interests in the Florida backwoods, for the peace and beauty I've found there have been definitely an escape from the confusion of our generation. You have faced the music and it is a symphony of discord" [MKR to FSF n.d. (October ?) 1936]. Of course, rural people, including crackers in the scrub, are not necessarily any more "simple" than anyone else, but her tendency to see them in this fashion explains why so few of her fictional characters are convincing human beings. Penny Baxter and Jody are two notable exceptions, possibly because both are to an important degree projections of her own character and thus acquire a psychological depth and complexity not to be found in her other characters.

She told Perkins, after reading Henry James' *The Art of the Novel*, "My writing is too personal a thing. The artist like de Maupassant or James can do a good job with any subject, any 'germ' as James calls it. I can only work with something that is of intense personal interest" [MKR to MEP November 17, 1934]. Undoubtedly this is one reason why *The Yearling* succeeded so well. According to her own statement, the book had its ultimate origins in her own childhood. In a piece she wrote to be broadcast overseas in a Voice of America series entitled "In This I Believe," she had this to say about the book's beginnings: "I remember a very special sort of April day, the day I describe in the first chapter of *The Yearling*. I remember the delirious excitement I felt. And at the height of my delight, a sadness came over me, and I understood suddenly that I should not always be a child, and that beyond this carefree moment life was waiting with its responsibilities. The feeling was so strong that I never forgot it. As I became a writer, I thought back often to that April day and that emotion, and I said to myself, 'Sometime I shall write a story about the job of childhood, and the strange foreknowledge of maturity.' "

She had the same intense personal commitment to the subject matter of *Cross Creek*. When she said in court at the "Cross

Creek Trial" that the book was a love song, of her love for Florida, she meant it quite literally. By the time she began writing this book in 1940 her apprenticeship was entirely behind her and she wrote as a first-rate literary craftsman, a true professional in full command of a significant talent. The measure of her growth as artist can be had by comparing this book with "Cracker Chidlings" where she was using almost identical materials. If the early piece was journalism, *Cross Creek* is literary art which bears comparison with Thoreau's *Walden*. In this book as in *The Yearling* circumstances combined to release her finest powers. She was dealing with material which she knew and loved deeply, but she had also learned the necessity for the right degree of artifice, the necessity to dominate "the facts" with imagination. She started with copious notes and sketches and she wrote in the vein of personal anecdote, lyric nature description, and earnest meditation in which she felt most at home. Her basic problem was to find a way to homogenize these materials into some kind of artistic whole. She wrote four drafts of the book over a period of nearly two years trying to discover the proper key.

Though it started out to be a book about a place, before she was done it had become quite as much a book about people. She wrote about real people whom she knew well, and whom she therefore did not conceive of as "characters" to be looked at as either simple or complicated. But she shaded her account of each of these people so that in effect she presents a large number of unusually vivid personalities who are based on real people but who are also quite as much fictive creations. She describes George Fairbanks like this: "He has an aloofness, a central integrity, that is his heritage from his good blood. He is the last of a once proud and prosperous line. The great Fairbanks family itself has been sifted by time and circumstance until only George is left to carry the name. He carries it in an amazing body, bony and gangling, with no chin at all, a black mustache, the whole dressed loosely in nondescript garments topped by an immense black Stetson hat. The effect is a parody of the villain in an old-fashioned melodrama. He is gentleness itself, except when corn liquor inflames him and the Fairbanks blood runs hot, and stuttering, he tells any man on earth what he thinks of him" [*CC*, 125-26].

Mr. Swilley she met when she stumbled over him unexpectedly one morning on the way to the barn: "He looked like a cross between an Indian and one of those travelling quacks known as medicine men. He had dark cavernous eyes, high cheekbones and lank black hair that hung to his shoulders. I found later that he cut his own hair and was dependent for even this rudimentary barbering on the loan of some one's scissors. . . . I learned in time to make some preliminary noise whenever I approached him, preferably some natural woods noise such as the breaking of a stick, for if I called or spoke or came unexpectedly within his vision, he cried out in that grunting pain and jerked like a monkey on a stick. He lived most of the time, I think, in a trance, and I have wondered from what strange and lovely world I brought him unhappily back to life" [*CC*, 128].

She wrote of a number of the long train of Negroes who worked for her in house or grove. One of the most memorable of these was 'Geechee: "The black girl came on foot the four miles from the village. She was barefooted. She strode up the path to the back door, thick-legged, her big toes splayed in the sand. She stopped short and glared at me, as though she meant to strike me. She wore one garment, too short for her erect height. It was of muslin flour sacking, so tattered that the full length of one sweating thigh showed through its multiple rents. She was the dusty black of teakwood. Two short tufts of hair were braided over her temples. They were stiff, a trifle curved, like horns."

Marjorie's characterizations proceeded as much by dialogue and dramatic action as by straight description:

She said fiercely, "I hear tell you want a girl. You take me."
She seemed impossible. She looked capable of murder. It would be like having a black leopard loose in the house.
I said, "I wanted a young girl."
"I be's young."

"No. One young enough to teach my ways."

"If I don't do to suit you, you can cut my throat."

[Marjorie was at last browbeaten into trying the girl, who now turned to go back to get her things in the village.]

She was gone, striding down the path toward some black and Amazonian army that awaited her coming that the battle might begin. I felt dazed and foolish, as though I had been hypnotized by a grotesque idol. She was the ugliest Negress I had ever seen. . . . As the weeks passed I bought her a cautious cheap uniform or two. Even in their white formality she seemed always about to burst into a belligerent dance, tearing her garments from her, prancing naked in a savage triumph. The effect came from her lioness stride, from her unkempt hair which shot in black spirals from her skull, and from the white eye with its hypnotic probing. She had been blind in it, she said, since the big fight.

"I dis-remember did I get the lick before they put me in the jailhouse or en-durin' the time they was puttin' me in the jailhouse" [CC, 82-84].

'Geechee turned out to be a hardworking and loyal servant and also a loving friend whose affection Marjorie heartily returned, but 'Geechee also had a helpless affection for a sorry man and an unquenchable thirst for alcohol, so that the chapter Marjorie devotes to this strangely appealing woman is an account full of humor, love, and pathos—all three.

There was always a hint of the *grande dame*, of the lady of the manor, in Marjorie's stance toward Negroes, but this was no more than a small corner of her attitude, and something she was probably entitled to as owner of a substantial property which constantly needed hired help. For the most part she looked toward Negroes with an unusual candor which was both clear-eyed and charitable, and she wrote of them with a combination of frankness and sympathy. She had almost none of the self-conscious patronizing sentimentality of the official do-gooder, and none of the common prejudices. For these reasons, her portraits of Negroes in this book carry unusual conviction. She is always pointing her account to make a good story but she is usually telling something close to the truth as she saw it.

Her literary treatment of Martha Mickens, the old Negro woman with the "face like poured chocolate" who worked for Marjorie and lived in the tenant house off and on for years, is noteworthy. Aunt Martha was in real life a pleasant and handsome elderly woman with an alert mind and warm, engaging personality who was wise in many ways with the wisdom of age, but she was by no means the sage nor the aristocratic social arbiter of the local Negro community which Marjorie represents her as being. While Marjorie was struggling to find a proper way to bind together the diverse elements of this book, she sent a part of the second draft to Perkins, who wrote back suggesting that she think of the book as "a single piece of string with knots in it, the knots being the episodes, but each connected with the other by incidents." He also suggested the talk of the Negroes and a cycle of the four seasons as other unifying devices. Marjorie found no way to run a central thread of narrative, though she used a rough progression of events from early years to late, but she did use a sequence of four chapters treating the four seasons and she made extensive use of the Negroes, particularly of Martha, as a kind of shuttle to weave together the various strands of the book, so that in the book she is given a prominence far greater than she actually had in Marjorie's life at the Creek. Marjorie sometimes lets herself grow lyric in the passages treating Martha: "The colored population of the Creek has the solid base of the Mickens family, against which other transient Negroes surge and retreat. When Old Martha Mickens shall march at last through the walls of Jericho, shouting her Primitive Baptist hymns, a dark rock at the core of the Creek life will have been shattered to bits. She is nurse to any of us, black or white, who fall ill. She is mid-wife and layer out of the dead. She is the only one who gives advice to all of us impartially. She is a dusky Fate, spinning away at the threads of our Creek existence" [*CC*, 17].

Such rhapsodic utterances occur less often than homely, intimate anecdotes involving Martha, so that she emerges, like most other people treated in the book, a completely convincing person. But the little edge of artifice, the coloring and shading which all are given, makes these persons true literary creations rather than documentary photographs casually snapped from life.

Marjorie found her greatest problem with the book to be one of presenting the material in such a way that the reader would see incident from the same point of view and in the same depth as she did. A simple day-to-day running narration, she found, came out flat and lacking the immediacy she wanted. "It's not enough for good anecdotes to be told," she wrote to Perkins. "The sense of knowing a particular place and people with a deep, almost Proustian deepness and intimacy and revelation, with my own feeling about things back of it is what I want. . . . To do it as I have begun the last time, is like doing hard creative fiction. I can call less on facts and true details, and must project myself painfully and slowly into years and scenes and feelings that I have actually forgotten, and must recreate. I would say that I cannot do it, except that I know by working hard enough, it is possible. . . . We cannot talk of illustrations or any publishing matters. The book can only be done right, no matter how long it takes" [MKR to MEP March 3, 1941]. Here undoubtedly the artist has taken commanding precedence over the reporter, and composing over telling.

In the final analysis, the combining ingredient which brought together all the disparate elements in this book was her own personality, and the pastoral attitude we have already mentioned. One has the sense that she has put herself on record in this book much as Whitman or Thoreau had done in their books a hundred years earlier, believing as they did that the best approach to the universal is through the particular and personal. Her candor and earthiness are visible here, her intelligence and humor and grit, her imagination and sensitivity to the beauty in common things, her mystic streak, her sympathy for other people. She had just lived through the ten most significant years of her life, had made a name and a considerable fortune by writing a book which nearly everyone hailed as a classic, and she had done this without tricks, by a slow, painful growth through several earlier books in which she struggled patiently to make words hold and project something like the beauty of her own vision. So she looked out upon her world at this moment of her life with a confidence in her powers and a sense of her own worth, with a modest but sure equilibrium, which she would never have again. She wrote without vanity of her own personal experience of the ten years past, and gave without coyness her own philosophy of life, confident that both were meaningful and that people would be genuinely interested to read about them.

Cross Creek was the last chapter in her prolonged account of her experience with Florida. After this she turned deliberately away to begin the struggle with *The Sojourner*, and to encounter again, almost as if she were starting her whole apprenticeship once more, the vexing enigma of how to place the fulcrum of her story at the proper point between fact and fiction. Her theoretical conviction about the need for creative re-working of fact to produce true literature never changed, but the body of fact itself and her larger artistic intention did change. *Cross Creek* worked out well eventually because she *knew* so much. The Proustian depth she sought, and in the main achieved, was possible only in the presence of an exhaustive knowledge and personal experience of the subject, and in this case she knew enough so that she could seek for concentrated essence of place and people without ever coming close to the limit of her grasp of the material—without ever having to formulate basic substance from her own imagination.

With *The Sojourner* it was quite different. Far from having a large stock of personal experience on which to draw, she had to construct by prolonged research and imaginative effort something like the entire fabric of farm life in the Middle West of two generations earlier. Her whole instinct was still that of the regionalist, the realist of place, only she had shifted regions and now had to absorb enough of a new place and way of life to give a convincing replica. For another thing, she conceived of *The Sojourner* from the very beginning as a doctrinaire book. Ase Linden was to be an Everyman who had her own "cosmic consciousness" and through whom she meant to convey her own mature understanding of human life and destiny. So the book had theme and to spare.

As she began, she might well have congratulated herself that in this book at least she would not be overwhelmed by the facts, though this turned out not to be the case. In her search for material she turned inward to personal reminiscence and to her own family's experience in southern Michigan seventy-five years earlier. The subject had the same antiquarian appeal which had drawn her to *The Yearling*, and under the notion that it would lend authenticity she used her own grandfather Traphagen as the prototype for Ase. This grandfather had been a subject of fascination for her for years. She had written a long poem based on the man while she was still an undergraduate at Wisconsin. In August of 1943 on the way back to Florida after seeing Norton off in New York on his voyage to India to serve with the American Field Service, she made a wide circle out to Michigan to visit her Aunt Ethel Riggs, who had boxes full of the grandfather's letters and ledgers. This mass of new information gave her a surge of enthusiasm for the new book. She was electrified by one entry in particular in her great-grandfather's account book, a note of receipt for a book on astronomy which she presumed her grandfather would have read in detail, and this gave her a thrill of conviction that he actually *had* been a person of "cosmic consciousness." She eagerly ordered a copy of the book from a Chicago bookstore because she thought it would give her exact knowledge of the man's cosmic awareness. But all of her immersion in family records proved to be a major tactical blunder—a new enslavement to facts. Five months later, after two unsuccessful attempts to get the book going, she wrote to Perkins in near-despair: "The book haunts me, I wake up in the night and think about it, and I do not know whether I simply am not ready, or whether my general mental distraction is to blame. . . . For one thing, I think it has been necessary to shake free from the facts and true characters that first suggested the book to me. The truth was not making me free but was chaining me. I shall do better to keep the basic conception and use more imagination in dealing with the characters. My subject matter is too big for me and my only salvation will be in working slowly and carefully. I seem faced with a great block of marble from which I must chip out, fragment by fragment, my concept" [MKR to MEP January 13, 1944]. Eight years later she was still chipping painfully away at the block to which her literary ambition and sheer stubborn determination kept her chained. She was not far wrong in believing that the subject was too big for her; she tried to do too much in the book.

In basic plot the story was simple: Ben, the older of the two Linden brothers, handsome, irresponsible, profligate, takes the share of money that falls to him at his father's death and goes off to seek a larger fortune in the West. Asahel, the younger, stays at home and works the family farm, still owned by Amelia the mother, who hates Ase and thinks only of Benjamin's return. Ase marries Nellie, Ben's sweetheart, raises a large family, improves the farm as he works it, and at last, nearly eighty years old, is summoned by a scrawled note to his brother's deathbed in a dingy waterfront rooming house in San Francisco. The brothers have a brief reconciliation before Ben dies and conveys to Ase the deed to the farm which he has worked a whole lifetime and never sought ownership of. Ase in turn conveys the farm to the son of Polish immigrants, so that the farm will be properly cared for after his death, since his own children are given over to the most rapacious and corrupt capitalist greed. On the flight home from San Francisco, Ase dies in a scene reminiscent of Hemingway's "Snows of Kilimanjaro."

As we have already seen in a previous chapter, Marjorie attempts in this book to give a major restatement of the American dream, in a fully developed version of the pastoral myth of the ideal husbandman tilling the fertile garden of the symbolic middle landscape. This includes an intense polemic against modern bourgeois materialism, which she pictures as subverting and devouring the American nation. She also meant the book to have suggestive overtones of the story of Job, the man who suffers in silence; and she meant the book, finally, to be a statement of her own deepest penetration into the meaning of human life and destiny. For a vehicle to carry such heavy freight of serious idea, she fell back on the form traditionally used for this purpose in Protestant culture, the allegory, so that in spite of a surface realism detailing many aspects of farm life in the Middle West in the late nineteenth century, most of the major actions in the book and virtually all of the characters also exist at the symbolic level. Ase contains something of Everyman, Job, Abraham Lincoln, and a Fisher Indian. He is the inarticulate man of infinite patience, the man of quiet brotherly love, the ideal husband, the ideal farmer, a free spirit known truly only to persons outside the Establishment—to a drunken Irishman, a band of gypsies, and to his spiritual father, Mink, the last of the Fisher Indians. He is generous, kindly, wise, a frustrated musician, philosopher, and scholar; he is literally his brother's keeper, keeping the farm for him without murmur for three-quarters of a century; he is a good Physiocrat in his reverence for the land and his refusal to own any of it; he is a Seeker, a spiritually sensitive believer in the cosmic consciousness. His mother Amelia is a hard, selfish, narrow woman symbolic of the dominant American Puritanism of the past. She hates music, art, and physical beauty and pleasure in any form; she hates Ase and everything he represents and is fanatically devoted with a possessive love to her profligate Benjamin. Ase's wife Nellie is the brisk, pert, pretty, capable American housewife and mother, cheerful, well-adjusted, pragmatic, materialistic, uncomplicated, completely at home in this world. Most of his children are monstrous devotees of Mammon who inherit materialism from both mother and grandmother. One little daughter, Doll, who truly loves him and is his kindred spirit, is destroyed when she is led off by the demented Amelia and lost in a blizzard.

Like other allegories, the book displays a high degree of artifice. The characters are almost all types, if not personified abstractions. Though generally somber, the book is ultimately affirmative. Because of the natural wisdom imparted to him by his Indian "father," Ase is enabled to resist both the harsh puritan narrowness of his mother (the past) and the degenerate materialism of his son (the future) and save the American land from pollution by conveying it to his true heir, the still uncorrupted descendant of immigrants. Because of his intuitive awareness, Ase is at one with his environment, labors lovingly in the earth, takes life's joys with gratitude and its pains with stoic courage. He lives with complete integrity and dies after a long life, with his spirit soaring outward into the cosmos on an upward trajectory.

The book represents a noble attempt to write the great American novel, but it must be counted more of a failure than a success—even when read as allegory rather than as realist fiction. The plot is forced, the characters wooden, the prose often sententious and turgid. From the very beginning Marjorie was working with too large an ambition in an alien mode. Like all other writers, she used symbols, but except in this last novel and in a few of the late short stories she was not a conscious symbolist in the sense that Joyce or Faulkner was. She had no gift for the subtleties, ambiguities, and ironies required of sustained symbolism, and her natural warmth and colloquial informality were smothered in this last novel by her self-conscious attempt to adopt the symbolic mode.

One of her greatest assets in the Florida writings was her style—open, energetic, vividly humane. Two things happened to release Marjorie's literary potential—the first was her discovery of Florida and the second was her learning from Hemingway the use of the blunt declarative sentence. She never acknowledged a specific debt, but there seems little question that in the late twenties or early thirties she went to school to Hemingway like so many other writers of her generation. In any case her style underwent a radical change, from overwritten journalese to a relatively chaste, unadorned style. Her college writings were undistinguished—earnest, sententious, full of "literary" mannerisms. The notes she took on first coming to Florida showed the same straining for effect: "The roof leaked erratically, like a woman who cries for nothing at all. Door sills wavered and were denied help. Steps wore off at the edges, like an old hag's teeth." Replying to one of her old colleagues on the Wisconsin *Lit* who had expressed surprise and delight at her first Florida pieces, she said, "The type of writing that is natural to me—quick, splashy, overwritten—is bad writing. It has taken me all these years to learn to work under my own thumb screws. If I let go the least bit, I can still turn out the most hopeless mess you would wish to see" [MKR to Ernest L. Meyer n.d. (1932)]. This was accurate enough. The will to discipline was her own, but there can be little doubt that she learned from Hemingway the direction in which to move.

As early as "Jacob's Ladder" the Hemingway manner is discernible in her writings: "The girl was awakened by the tumult. It was broad day, and the outer perimeter of the hurricane was moving across the section. The yellow-grayness of the sky was tinged with green in the west. The roar of the wind was a train thundering nearer and nearer. The palmettos thrashed their fans in a frenzy. Rain was pounding on the roof as though it would beat it open. On the gutters it flailed like bird-shot. . . .

"Sport darted into the kitchen, his spotted coat blown into bristles. He whimpered. He was always afraid in a storm. She set the plate of cornbread on the floor and he gulped it, his ribs heaving in and out. He came back to her, quivering. She listened for sounds from old Jo. She could hear nothing in the tumult . . ." [*WTW*, 49]. Signs of Hemingway influence are detectable throughout her writings, and the debt was large and important, but she was too independent and too fundamentally different in outlook and personality for the manner ever to become slavish.

As we have seen, she made extensive and masterful use of dialect, but most of her stories except for the comic stories are narrated in third person in a voice which uses standard, and at times formal, language. In the early stories this sometimes resulted in a clash of tones, as in the following passage from *South Moon Under* where Lant and his cousin Cleve dispute amiably about the risks of 'gatoring:

"Don't you fret about me and the 'gatoring'," [Cleve] *said. "Wilsons and Saunders has wanted I should go with 'em. Not me."*

" 'Tain't no risk to it."

"Don't tell me. How come Nub-Footed Turner lost half his foot if they ain't no risk?"

"He were jest keerless."

"I might git keerless, too. I'm ridin' range for Uncle Ab and savin' a dollar-two a week. I aim to keep away from 'gators right on."

[Then immediately following this easy-going dialect comes the author's voice in a formal expository tone.]

Towards the end of the summer the larger saurians were seldom seen. The females prepared for the September hatching of the eggs, laid in the spring, and hunted winter quarters. They were already holing up here and there in deep watery caves in swamp and river-bed. They had been decimated by the spring and summer hunting. The remaining adults added an acquired wariness to an instinctive one [*SMU*, 183].

By the time she began *The Yearling*, she had learned to avoid such discrepancies and the style flows out with seamless integrity. In the early short stories she had learned to use several variations of stream of consciousness, and this book comes chiefly as a sequence of revelations to the alert, yet open and wondering mind of twelve-year-old Jody Baxter. To reveal Jody's inner consciousness she uses, not the cloud of impressions of Joyce or Virginia Woolf, the layered accumulation of thought upon thought, sense upon sense, but a modified third-person record of this process. She can thus be highly selective, can give a direct impression of Jody's mind or an edited version which includes his reaction to some impression, or she can move entirely outside the inner world of Jody's consciousness to interpretation or commentary or detached exposition. The final paragraph of chapter one illustrates the versatility of the method. She starts on the outside by echoing a remark of Ma Baxter, who has said to Jody:

"You're addled. . . . Jest plain addled."

It was true. He was addled with April. He was dizzy with Spring. He was as drunk as Lem Forrester on a Saturday night. His head was swimming with the strong brew made up of the sun and the air and the thin gray rain. The flutter-mill had made him drunk, and the doe's coming, and his father's hiding his absence, and his mother's making him a pone and laughing at him. He was stabbed with the candle-light inside the safe comfort of the cabin; with the moonlight around it. He pictured old Slewfoot, the great black outlaw bear with one toe missing, rearing up in his winter bed and tasting the soft air and smelling the moonlight, as he, Jody, smelled and tasted them. He went to bed in a fever and could not sleep. A mark was on him from the day's delight, so that all his life, when April was a thin green and the flavor of rain was on his tongue, an old wound would throb and a nostalgia would fill him for something he could not quite remember. A whip-poor-will called across the bright night, and suddenly he was asleep [*Y*, 14-15].

In this passage she gradually moves down into Jody's consciousness to his recall of the day's events which had contributed to his feeling of intoxication with spring, until she registers directly a thought about the great bear. Then she moves back up out of Jody's consciousness to objective commentary ending on a lyric note.

The second chapter shows a similar skill with the method. The chapter begins as a record of Penny Baxter's thoughts as he lies in bed on this same moonlight night, thoughts which modulate to a third-person exposition providing necessary background information about Penny's past and his reasons for coming to live in the scrub, and then modulating back into a direct register of his thoughts. This mode of narration allows Marjorie to expand or contract her field of vision, to move back and forth in time, liberties which she uses sparingly, preferring to remain focused most of the time on carefully realized action in the present moment.

Her use of this point of view accords perfectly with the tone she meant to strike between realistic presentation of an actual world with its sights and sounds and smells, and an idyllic sense of wonder with which a twelve-year-old looked out upon this world. This compromise was the hardest thing of all in writing the book, and she went back time after time to prune out a softness which crept into the style. As late as the galley proofs she was still revising. "In reading the whole thing as a unit," she told Perkins, "I realize that the [idyllic] quality, almost an indefinable one, is pervasive of the complete book, for the reason that the quality was actually a salient ingredient in my own feeling. . . . The first chapter, which is idyllic, is keyed as I intended, originally, to key the whole thing. I was disturbed when I found the boy becoming so actual, fearing disharmony. Whether the quality is more valuable than the idyllic quality is perhaps a debatable question. But I do see the story within myself, poetically, and I'm afraid there is no getting away from it, even when there is too much of it. But there are many places which need a greater stiffness, and I shall supply it whenever I can" [MRK to MEP January 23, 1938].

Robert Frost spoke of two kinds of realist in literature, the one who offers a good deal of dirt with his potato to show that it is a real potato, and the one who is satisfied with the potato brushed clean. Marjorie was a realist of the second kind, but one should add that her brushing-clean often included a considerable editing of the reality she presented. She reminds one in this respect of the American genre painters of the last century like William S. Mount or George Caleb Bingham, who painted scenes from actual life, especially rural scenes, with a smooth, brightly lighted realism, but a cleaned-up realism which omitted the sordid and most forms of the ugly, gave a uniform pleasantry to their human subjects, and cast over the whole a nostalgia for a simpler, happier time now receded into the past. The reality which Marjorie depicts is much like this, particularly in the period pieces like *The Yearling*, except that there is less cheeriness because she also adds a considerable mixture of the darker tones of human anguish. Reading the book, one has the sense of experiencing a full life until he begins to enumerate the areas of experience which are omitted: most forms of human depravity and violence; virtually all sexual experience; almost all forms of social intercourse; the entire realms of politics, education, religion, and other forms of institutional life; except at a remote distance, there is in the book no nation, no state, and no city. She has deliberately restricted the subject, as we have previously noted, to a pastoral microcosm, a family living in a garden surrounded by the wilderness. Her entire focus is upon their elemental struggle to survive, and upon the elemental processes of human growth and decay. A boy, and his relation of love to his father, to the animal world and the world of nature; a father, with his patient fostering love for his child, his courage and great skill in providing for his family; the pain of irretrievable loss and of alienation from loved ones; the joy of reconciliation. No subject matter could be more universal, and none more fraught with peril of the obvious or the sentimental. This is the "what oft was thought" of the classicist, and because of the unrelenting discipline through which she gave it needed chastity and rigor, one is tempted to add, "ne'er so well express'd."

Cross Creek was a similar triumph of style in which, using very different means and materials, she brought off a second time the precarious idyllic tone she had sought in *The Yearling*. Her intention, in her own words, was that "readers would be taken into a totally strange world, and that they would feel a certain delight and enchantment in the strangeness" [MKR to MEP October n.d., 1941]. In the first draft, each sketch took the form of a little gem of prose, elegant and a bit formal, but she soon discovered that the material itself was so informal that it demanded a simple conversational style, and this is the way she finally wrote it—as if talking in a direct and friendly way to a reader about her life at the Creek. Because of the familiar tone, she was able in this book to make freest use of her gifts as raconteur, and she pours out anecdote after anecdote in a deceptively easy flow, story mixed with lyric nature description, character sketch with serious meditation, and the whole permeated by her own humanity and a bright glint of humor.

How much did Marjorie Kinnan Rawlings achieve of the place in American literature for which she fought so hard? Harry Bernard, in his study of the American regional novel, called *The Yearling* the masterpiece among regional novels of today [*Le Roman Régionaliste aux Etats-Unis* (Montreal, 1949), 138] but this kind of accolade from a serious critic is unusual. Marjorie has suffered an almost total neglect by critics. Her popular reputation shows an unusual curve: She went from total obscurity in 1933 to something like international acclaim in 1939; then enjoyed a high plateau of public favor until the middle forties; then suffered a sloping off until her death in 1953 when, as is not uncommon, she dropped back into semi-obscurity. This is all with respect to the intellectual and critical world as well as the so-called general reading public. At another level, not always highly esteemed by the official literary world, she continues to maintain a steady following, and that is among juvenile readers. *The Yearling* continues to sell thousands of copies year after year, particularly in the school edition, and one could confidently predict that this trend would continue into the indefinite future—a fate this book shares with *Gulliver's Travels, Huckleberry Finn, Treasure Island,* and other books which the world has long called "classics."

It is probable that Marjorie's popularity reached a higher peak in the early forties than she deserved, and probably as much from the tom-toms of press agentry as from the intrinsic worth of her writings. One adoption by a national book club has a way of leading on to another (four out of her five longer works were adopted by Book-of-the-Month or Literary Guild). But making best-seller lists is an ephemeral distinction, a kind of kudos which has little to do with an author's true worth. Marjorie's gift was not a major one like Faulkner's and yet she outsold him for the better part of ten years. In 1940 *The Yearling* was enough in public consciousness that MGM assigned their most expensive talent to do the film version—Spencer Tracy as Penny Baxter, Marc Connelly as script writer, Victor Fleming as director. These arrangements fell through partly because of dislocations caused by the war and the film was set aside until 1945, when it was rescheduled with Gregory Peck as Penny, Jane Wyman as Ma Baxter, and Claude Jarman as Jody.

The film went so well that MGM approached Marjorie with a proposal to do a script for the super-dog Lassie in which they could capitalize on Claude Jarman's success as Jody in *The Yearling*. Carl Brandt, her literary agent, urged her to rewrite and expand an earlier story, "Mother in Mannville," which she did, producing a novel-length fiction entitled "Mountain Prelude." Brandt immediately sold magazine rights to *The Saturday Evening Post,* where it ran in six installments beginning in April, 1947. This was pure hack-work, a pot-boiler which Marjorie turned out almost cynically, too deeply involved now in the rat race of the big-time to be able to say no to the sixty thousand dollars it netted her. She can hardly be blamed for spreading her apron to the golden fruit which now fell almost of its own accord from the tree she had shaken for so many years without result. Actually, for someone whose name could ring the nation's cash registers, she did very little of this kind of hack-work —a preface or two, an encyclopedia article on the craft of writing, a magazine article urging conservation of the nation's timber resources. By far the greatest share of her literary energies were committed to serious literature.

She earned the right to be called a dedicated spirit. She made such demands on herself, and the writing came so hard, that she often spoke of being "doomed" to write. She made mistakes of judgment, as in *Golden Apples,* but she paid blood tribute to the muse for every piece she wrote, and she did not often flinch from the sternest demands of an acute artistic conscience. She sat on the porch at Cross Creek in a cowhide chair at the round table supported by a palm-log column, or she lay propped up on pillows in bed with the portable typewriter across her lap, and she put in the time. Her newspaper days loosened her flow of words somewhat and taught her to compose on the typewriter, but she always wrote painfully, often having only a few lines to show for a day's effort. She worked the whole day and, when pressed, on into the night, but usually broke off in the late afternoon for drinks and dinner, and then read nonfiction in the evening.

Marjorie was fifty-seven when she died, and the last twenty-five years of her life saw a steady commitment to literary art. The commitment netted one novel, *The Yearling,* which shows all the signs of being a classic (and more than one literary reputation has rested upon a single book) but there was more in Marjorie's case. *Cross Creek* is a second book which may well become a classic for qualities which have generated a worshipful following for Thoreau's *Walden*, a book it resembles in important ways. To these, as a third portion of her work having the highest literary value, should be added the four comic short stories: "Alligators," "Benny and the Bird Dogs," "Varmints," and "Cocks Must Crow." A cut under these works, but still having a high degree of literary worth, come the regional stories: *South Moon Under*, "Jacob's Ladder," "Gal Young Un," and "Plumb Clare Conscience."

This is not major literary achievement, not as one compares it to the achievement of Faulkner or Hemingway, but it is substantial. Arnold Bennett once described the novelist as the man who, "having seen life, and being so excited by it that he absolutely must transmit his vision to others, chooses narrative fiction as the liveliest vehicle for the relief of his feelings." This precisely describes the Marjorie Kinnan Rawlings of the Florida stories. In these she had a vision of life which she *had* to transmit, a pastoral vision of singular beauty and appeal. In a time when it was fashionable to be negative and despairing, her books were affirmative. In a time of great social and economic distress, of moral confusion and uncertainty, her stories quietly reasserted a familiar American ethic. In the heyday of the anti-hero, her Penny Baxter was an unobtrusive but true hero of the traditional sort. His virtues in abstraction sound like a rehearsal of the Boy Scout code—he was loyal, brave, honest, kindly, generous, and all the rest—but he was also sternly self-reliant and stoically tough. Her Jody Baxter undergoes a shattering of innocence not unlike that of Hemingway's Nick Adams figures or the young men in Sherwood Anderson's stories, but he comes to a much more satisfactory settlement with life's painful demands than they do. Hemingway's young men do not often recover from their "unreasonable wound," but go into a stasis or a flight to the wilderness or into frantic hedonism to escape a confrontation too painful to be lived with. Jody returns to Baxter's Island where he takes up manly responsibility for the family's support.

It will not do to read down Marjorie's achievement because of what she did not do. There was no Eve in her Florida Eden, and the snake there did not represent temptation but only sudden death. Jody's passage into maturity did not come through any fall from sexual innocence, but from an agony of alienation from a beloved father and from an encounter with Death and Starvation. Leslie Fiedler, with good cause, has accused the classic American novelists of being unable to depict mature heterosexual love or to create full-bodied female characters of the order of Thackeray's Becky Sharp. In this respect, Marjorie certainly belongs with her predecessors in the American tradition. She produced *no* female character of distinction, except Quincy Dover, and seemed totally incapable of portraying relationships between the sexes. This is an undoubted limitation, but she did with surpassing excellence something else for which her American background may have peculiarly fitted her—she gave one of literature's most convincing portrayals of childhood innocence, and her portrayal is the more convincing because it is without softness. Nothing is more central to her statement than a tragic awareness that a boy's world contains loneliness as well as beauty and pain as well as purity, that innocence cannot last, and that its shattering is accompanied by a hard anguish. The pastoral vision in her books is of a world of natural beauty free from the stench and ugliness of modern cities, but it also includes Penny's stoic conviction that life will inevitably knock a man down, and when it does a man takes this for his share and goes on. This kind of pastoralism is neither an invitation to dalliance under the yum-yum tree nor to a wallowing in the pit of existentialist despair. Such a balanced view of human existence is more traditional than modern, and one might even say, more "classic."

Like the great romantics, Wordsworth, Emerson, and Whitman, Marjorie's special vision was for the beauty and magic in the commonplace, but her range was limited. She needed the specific stimulus of experience to spark her imagination, and not any personal experience would do. Only the Florida years seemed to be viable artistically. She was unable, like Henry James or Faulkner or other writers of highest imaginative power, to find stimulus in an almost indefinite range of human life.

Once Marjorie had written of Florida, there was nothing else in her life which stirred her with the same compelling urge to creative effort. *The Sojourner* was written compulsively, but more from literary ambition than from a vision of life which demanded expression. Even with its northern setting it contains nothing substantially different from the statement of the earlier writings, and remains a kind of porch to the main edifice of the Florida books.

Within her limited range Majorie shows the uniqueness and the authority of the true artist. All her writings have the important virtue of readability, and in this respect she belongs to the older great tradition of Twain and Howells rather than to the modern school which began with Henry James. She will probably continue to be more a reader's writer than a critic's writer since the special virtues of her books are more readily experienced than described. She may not have notched as high nor as big a blaze on the pine tree of literary fame as she hoped, but the mark that she made was deep and will last.

Index

Index

Index

A
GILCHRIST
TRENTON
DIXIE
N
SUWANNEE RIVER
WACASSASSA RIVER
LEVY
0
10
20
30

213780

Bigelow, Gordon E.
Frontier Eden; the literary career of Marjorie Kinnan Rawlings, by Gordon E. Bigelow. Gainesville, University of Florida Press, 1972 [c1966]
xvii, 162 p. illus., map (on lining paper) ports. 24 cm.

1. Rawlings, Marjorie (Kinnan) 1896-1953. I. Title